NUTS AND BOLTS

NUTS AND BOLTS
SURVIVAL GUIDE FOR TEACHERS

CINDY J. CHRISTOPHER

TECHNOMIC
PUBLISHING CO., INC.
LANCASTER · BASEL

Nuts and Bolts
a **TECHNOMIC** publication

Published in the Western Hemisphere by
Technomic Publishing Company, Inc.
851 New Holland Avenue
Box 3535
Lancaster, Pennsylvania 17604 U.S.A.

Distributed in the Rest of the World by
Technomic Publishing AG

Printed in the United States of America
10 9 8 7 6 5 4 3 2 1

Main entry under title:
    Nuts and Bolts: Survival Guide for Teachers

A Technomic Publishing Company book
Bibliography: p. 129
Includes index p. 131

Library of Congress Card No. 91-66931
ISBN No. 87762-858-0

To my Mom, who has always been there for me as a source of inspiration, and who has taught me never to give up on my dreams and to live life to the fullest. Also to my grandmother, Helen Parker, who was so proud of me and couldn't wait to read this book, but passed away on January 21, 1991. Thanks for your confidence and memories, Grandma. I love you.

CONTENTS

FOREWORD

SEVERAL colleagues and I teach a course in classroom discipline which is now required of the more than 1,000 students at our college who are preparing to teach elementary and junior high school. In this course, Cindy Christopher recently gave a guest lecture which was essentially her book in miniature. Using real classroom examples, she described in sharp and vivid detail how to arrange a classroom and organize materials, how to make trouble-free transitions between activities, how to set up and operate interest centers, how to keep records, how to deal effectively with parents—all the things a teacher needs to know how to do, but which are rarely taught in college or contained in books.

My students found her presentation one of the high points of the course. "It did wonders for my confidence," wrote one young woman. "I now feel I know what to do when I walk into a classroom."

However, it is not only teachers-to-be who are looking for help in dealing with the demands of today's classrooms. As part of our college's "Teachers for the 21st Century" project, we recently asked a select group of teachers and school administrators, "What will teachers need to know to do their jobs effectively in the next century?" One elementary school principal from an affluent white-collar community responded:

> We are seeing more and more at-risk kids; children from dysfunctional families; children from remarried families with two sets of values; children from families where there's no support for getting their homework done. Many of our veteran teachers are having trouble dealing with the learning and emotional needs of these children. We need teachers who are prepared to make adjustments, who can cope with the diverse needs that children are bringing to the classroom.

The changing American family is a well-documented social phenomenon. Forty to fifty percent of children born in the 1970s will live in a one-parent home for part of their childhood. One of every three families headed by a single mother lives in poverty. By the mid-1980s, more than 1.5 million children were living with neither parent. In the last two decades, reported cases of child abuse have risen more than 400 percent.

The impact of these changes on children, and consequently on teachers, has been profound. Classrooms are increasingly heterogeneous. More and more children have special needs. Discipline problems are more common. "We see fewer children," said the principal quoted above, "who come to us with their emotional needs met and eager to learn."

Motivating children to learn, meeting their diverse needs, and managing their behavior are paramount among the difficult challenges facing teachers today. No book can make that job easy. But Cindy Christopher's *Nuts and Bolts* offers real, practical help. It shows how to run a well-organized classroom whose structure supports children and stimulates their learning. It will, I believe, be enthusiastically welcomed by new and experienced teachers alike.

Thomas Lickona
Professor, Education, Cortland College
Author, *Educating for Character*

PREFACE

EVER since I was a small child, I knew that more than anything I wanted to be a teacher. In 1976 I set off to reach that dream. I went to a small, two-year college first and then transferred to a four-year college (both in upstate New York) to complete my degree. Upon graduating in 1980 I decided to open a nursery school, where I spent seven years directing and teaching. I started with two students and ended with thirty.

I eventually decided to try my hand at elementary school teaching. In 1988 I started teaching third grade in a rural central New York school. It was exactly the type of community I wanted to teach in, small and very friendly.

I found the change overwhelming. As I spent the month of August in my classroom, I called bookstores and asked if there were any books on the market for beginning or new teachers. Again and again, I was told they had none. Questioning other teachers, I began to realize how great the need was for such a resource.

Having completed my coursework at the State University College at Cortland for my Master's Degree, I approached two professors, Dr. Thomas Lickona and Dr. Phil Silvino, and shared my idea with them about a special project. I wanted to write a book for teachers covering many of the practical areas not discussed in college classes, and the things no one thinks about until they are teaching. They both agreed it was a good idea, and I was on my way.

I interviewed teachers from all types of school districts, from kindergarten through sixth grade. I also sent out questionnaires to administrators, parents, and teachers.

Sorting through material gathered, I decided to include only information that would be beneficial and relevant to new teachers, teachers in training, and teachers already in the field. My goal was to keep the book precise and short enough that it could be read quickly and be kept nearby as a reference guide.

ACKNOWLEDGEMENT /////

I owe many people a big thank you, from those who supplied information to my proofreader Charlotte King, who, in between moving, always had time for me; Phyllis McElroy, who taught me how to use a computer and helped with the printing; Tom Lickona, who encouraged me to get this book published; and last to my mom, Jane, who patiently listened when I temporarily seemed to have writer's block, or just needed a boost of confidence. I should also give credit to my first year's class of twenty-four students who encouraged me, answered my questions, and eagerly shared their thoughts on various subjects discussed in this book. Your overwhelming support and feedback made me believe I could write this book.

I thank each and every one of you!

INTRODUCTION ////

CONGRATULATIONS! You have studied hard, sent out resumes, gone through nerve-wracking interviews, and have succeeded in obtaining a teaching job. Once you have had the chance to settle down, you may begin to feel overwhelmed. As a teacher you have been prepared throughout your college experience to teach academic subjects, but once you get into a classroom you find that this is just one facet of the total teaching picture. Where do you begin? How do you arrange the room? How do you keep and document records? How do you organize your day? What subject do you teach first? Math? Reading? Language? This guide will help answer these questions and deal with the many problems you may face in your first year of teaching. Material was gathered from fellow teachers, college courses, and workshops. Some came without original sources, but sources have been cited whenever possible.

The first year of teaching is tough, and you will feel that all you think about and do is school, school, school. There is so much to learn, new lessons to prepare, school policies to follow, parents to deal with, and records to be kept. Working with students is a never-ending process — a child is never finished learning. You cannot close the door and forget about school until the next morning. Sometimes you may even wonder why you chose the teaching profession, but believe me it does get better after that first year is behind you. The key is to stay on top of things and be organized.

I hope as you read this guide, it will help you to survive your first couple of years and give you a quick reference. Good luck to you as you begin educating our nation's youth!

1 /////Lesson Planning

ONE of the hardest areas for teachers is scheduling. When, where, and how do you fit everything in and cover it in ten months? To top it off, you must work around "extras" such as: specials, speech, the resource room, math and reading labs. To a new teacher this can be extremely frustrating and can create a lot of anxiety. This chapter will help by providing a step-by-step process for setting up a schedule, including examples of schedules for kindergarten through grade six, a review of objectives, and tips for being evaluated by administrators.

Setting Up a Schedule

The first step in setting up your schedule is to make a chart for Monday through Friday and block in all your "extras" as mentioned above. These must be done first as you cannot change these times. Your schedule must be built around them. This will allow you to see how much actual classroom time you have left for other subjects.

Before you can block in your academic subjects, take a look at the "total picture." Write down everything you are required to teach. I find it helpful to list the individual subjects along with the total number of units and chapters in each. This allows you to see on paper which subjects demand more time and must be done daily.

You are now ready to start blocking in each subject. The first two to block in are reading and math. All the teachers and administrators interviewed said that these two were the most important and must be covered daily in order to finish the material by year's end. It was also agreed that, if possible, students should be taught reading and math in the morning when they are freshest and most attentive. Reading gener-

1

ally takes 20 to 30 minutes per group and Math anywhere from 30 to 50 minutes, depending on the level you are teaching.

Next, block in your other subjects. The following time spans for each subject will provide you with guidelines to get started. Of course, with your class you may find you need more or less time. Spelling (15 to 25 minutes), Handwriting (15 to 20 minutes), and English (30 to 45 minutes). By now you will begin to see your schedule is filling up, and you still have Science and Social Studies. I saved these for last because they can be alternated every other day and integrated with other areas. For example, if you are studying butterflies: (1) Write a descriptive paragraph (English and Handwriting). (2) Make a stained glass butterfly (Art). (3) Measure lengths of different butterflies (Math).

If you are familiar with the "whole language" approach, then you know how much scheduling time you can save through this integrated curriculum planning. Briefly stated, whole language is the total integration of language into every aspect of the educational curriculum. This frees up your schedule, giving you more flexibility, because you are integrating subjects and not teaching them separately. For more information and books on whole language, see the resource section.

The above is a basic guideline. Talk with the other teachers at your grade level and find out what works best for them, or what things must be scheduled at the same time. They may even be willing to help in setting up your schedule. The bottom line, though, is that for the first month you will have to experiment to find which schedule works best for you. The best advice given to me was to work into the subjects a little at a time; otherwise, you will become overwhelmed. The first month is ideal for doing this because you have to settle your students down, set the guidelines, and do any testing required by your school.

Included in Appendix A are examples of schedules for kindergarten through sixth grade. These will give you an idea of what typical schedules might look like at the primary and intermediate levels.

Long- and Short-Range Planning

Once you have a basic daily schedule, you can begin to concentrate on the academics of each. You should formulate a long-range and a short-range plan to follow. Otherwise, you may find that April has arrived and you still have a lot of material to cover. Long-range planning will eliminate this and help keep you on target.

An example of a long-range plan for Science (we use the Heath Science Books, therefore the following is based on that) would be to take the book, see how many chapters there are and arrange them into months. Mine for Science looks like this:

September — Chapter 1 — Where Do Plants and Animals Live?
October   — Chapter 2 — Groups of Living Things
November   — Chapter 3 — A Community
December   — Chapter 6 — Stars
January   — Chapter 4 — Water Cycle
February   — Chapter 5 — The Changing Land
March   — Chapter 9 — What Do We Eat?
April   — Chapter 10 — How We Use What We Eat
May   — Chapter 7 — Machines at Work
June   — Chapter 8 — Using Electricity

The first year I went even further and wrote down all the experiments, concepts, and supplies I would need. I found this to be a waste of time because everything is right in the Science Teacher's Edition. Now I only list extra things I am teaching relating to that chapter, so I will not forget them. As you become more experienced and add other learning units of your own, you should make room in long-range planning to incorporate them. Short-range planning would look something like this:

Chapter 3
Nov. 1   — Pages 56–59
Nov. 3   — Experiment—Observing a Community
Nov. 7   — Pages 60–63
           Experiment—Green Plants and Sunlight
Nov. 9   — Pages 64–66
           Experiment—How Does Water Get to the
           Leaves?
Nov. 12 — Pages 67–70
           Experiment—Growing Bread Mold
Nov. 15 — Pages 71–73
Nov. 17 — Pages 74–78

Nov. 21 – Pages 79–86
Nov. 27 – Experiment – Observing Insects
Nov. 29 – Pages 87–92
Dec. 1 – Wrap-up and exam

When I do reading on a short-range plan I only do one week at a time, because I find alterations are needed. Having a long-range plan allows me to know exactly what I need to complete each month. It also gives me the flexibility to alter plans on a daily basis; to allow for such variables as movies and assemblies; but to know in the back of my mind where I must be at the end of the month.

Objectives

As you begin to put things in your plan book, you will notice there isn't much space to record your plans. You are going to have to keep things simple. Check with your principal ahead of time to see if there is a format you must follow. Due to the limitation of space, you cannot possibly write in all the objectives you wish to accomplish. List only the major objectives (see example below).

Monday
Math – TE 100, Workbook 100
Add 2 numbers, with more than 1 renaming/80% score
Reading – TE 95, Workbook 95
Introduce vocab. from chart, reinforce by acting out,
85% score on workbook page

Tuesday
Math – TE 101, Workbook 101
Add 2 or 3 numbers, with more than 1 renaming/80% score
Reading – TE 96–108
Students must read story and complete the
comprehension questions with an 85% score

Each of the Teacher's Editions lists the objectives the author wishes to accomplish. A word of caution: Do not stick solely to these manuals, as they can be hazardous to children's learning! Relying on them entirely allows no creativity, and no room for your own input.

Think of them as references, but develop your own lesson to accomplish your objectives.

At this point I think it is necessary to quickly review what objectives are. An objective describes the performance students must display before they can be considered competent. Robert F. Mager in his book, *Preparing Instructional Objectives*, states three reasons why objectives are important. "Objectives are useful in providing a sound basis (1) for the selection or designing of instructional content and procedures, (2) for evaluating or assessing the success of the instruction, and (3) for organizing the students' own efforts and activities for the accomplishment of the important instructional intents" (Mager, 1975, p. 6). In simple terms, teachers must know where they are going to before they can get there.

In order to write an objective, the following three items must be included:

(1) Performance—what the learner is expected to be able to do. Performance objectives are either overt or covert. Overt performances can be observed directly by the eye or ear. Covert performances are mental, internal, invisible, and cognitive in nature.

(2) Conditions—any conditions under which the performance is expected to occur.

(3) Criterion—how well the learner must complete a task for it to be acceptable. When preparing the criterion part of the objective, it is important to include a time limit, the quality, and/or accuracy.

The following objective would satisfy all three parts: Using a globe, the student should be able to correctly label on a desk map the seven continents and four oceans within fifteen minutes.

As you begin setting up objectives, ask yourself whether there is a need for instruction, or a reason for the learning to occur. Then you can begin stating your objectives in respect to where you are going, how to get there, and finally, whether you have arrived. Make sure your objectives are clearly stated and not unnecessarily wordy. Above all, know your subject matter before you try to teach your students.

It is very helpful to write your schedule for the day on a separate piece of paper. When you have the time frame in front of you, it is easier to follow the schedule and stay on target. I try to leave room in my plan book to jot down any notes concerning how the lesson went. Did it take more time than anticipated? Was it an easy concept? Hard?

Was the lesson well received by your students? Do you feel it was successful, or that it needed more work? Notes such as these will be extremely beneficial to you when you begin to plan for the next year. If you remember, I mentioned that there wasn't much room in your plan book, therefore where will you write such comments? My school uses Bardeen Plan-Registers, and I use the right page for daily assignments, to list objectives and assignments. The left-hand side I use to list any materials I may need, and usually there is room left where I add my comments. For example:

Monday
Math—Students had trouble with renaming when zeros were involved, lesson took a long time.

Tuesday
Math—Sue, Deb, John, Alex had major problems, needed to be retaught, cut assignment in half and stayed in time frame allowed.

Lesson Planning Tips

Listed below are some tips to help you in your lesson planning.

- Make sure your students are on task.
- If at the end of a lesson you find more students are off task, perhaps your lesson was too long or detailed, or you introduced too much.
- Keep your class actively involved in lessons—students learn more when they are "doing."
- Teach to all modes of learning: kinesthetic, visual, and auditory.
- Overplan, especially the first couple of years; otherwise, you end up with a lot of extra time on your hands.

As you begin each lesson, quickly review what was discussed the day before. A simple question such as, "Could someone tell me what we learned yesterday?" will suffice. At the end of the lesson do the same thing, but this time ask, "What did we learn today?" With older students you could have them tell a neighbor one thing they learned and vice versa. Allow what I call "wait time," which means that after you ask a question, count to ten and then have someone answer. This allows students the opportunity to answer because you are giving all of them time to think. You will find that the time it takes to ask these two simple review questions is very worthwhile as you assess whether your objectives have been met and the lesson understood. The beginning question gives students the chance to reflect on what was taught yesterday and see that today's lesson continues to expand upon that concept. Wrapping up the lesson helps students reinforce what was taught and end the lesson on a positive note.

Many teachers use the time when some students are at the resource room, band, etc., as an activity period. They work with students who need extra help, while the rest of the class may be working on homework, at centers, or doing individual projects.

A final note concerning daily lesson planning: Include a fun thing each day so students will like learning and want to come to school. In my classroom I also plan a fun activity for each month such as: a winter hot dog roast, snow fun day, popcorn party, etc. Students look forward to these extra things, and need to have a break from academics occasionally.

Planning for a Sub

One important area often overlooked includes planning for a substitute teacher. Failure to do so means either coming to school sick and trying to teach, or getting up very early and driving to school to leave plans. Many schools have teachers leave a folder containing plans in the office to be used in an emergency situation. Leaving good plans for a substitute is a must in order to make the day go smoothly and orderly for all. Having substitute-taught for a year, I can tell you that many teachers wrongly assume a substitute knows where everything is located inside as well as outside the classroom. Based on this experience, I leave detailed plans explaining everything in a folder. I assume nothing. Plans are kept simple, so the substitute can easily follow them. Items in the folder are:

- seating chart
- copy of lunch and attendance slip

- classroom procedure and rules
- fire escape routes
- three names of students who are dependable and helpful
- names of students who go for enrichment, resource, chorus, band, and so on
- schedule of specials
- daily plan and where Teacher's Editions are located
- games, activities, story starters, for extra leftover minutes

Being Observed

Most new teachers are observed several times throughout the year by an administrator. To say these observations are nerve-wracking would be an understatement. You feel as if your teaching position depends on the outcome of these observations. To help you plan and deliver your lesson, keep these points in mind:

- Don't plan to do too much, or cover more material than necessary to meet your objectives. Try to keep the lesson short.
- Don't plan a lesson that involves a new concept.
- Be aware of those students who are off-task and draw them back into the lesson. I find that instead of asking students to raise their hands after asking a question, randomly picking someone keeps the class much more alert. Also, asking students to rephrase what other students have said keeps the group involved and active. A simple "Could you tell me what Bill said?" will do it. Your goal is total class involvement rather than just individual involvement.
- Look around your room—is it a place children enjoy being in? Is it neat? Messy? Cluttered?
- Make sure your objectives are clear, and that you know how they will be met.
- Begin with an interesting introduction; get the students' attention right away and keep it.
- Try to have your observation in the morning when your class is fresh.
- End the lesson with the question, "What have we learned today?"

- Dress neatly and appropriately.
- Be positive in your approach, and smile. When you are enjoying what you are presenting, the students can sense this and take an interest in learning.
- Make sure you feel confident in your ability to teach the particular lesson you choose. Remember you will be nervous.

I have many problems with observations. I personally feel that if you are a good teacher, the things mentioned above should be done all the time. Too many teachers spend hours preparing for a visit; therefore, the administrator is not getting the "real" everyday classroom teacher and environment. Being a teacher is an important responsibility. There should be no room for those who appear to be competent on a few occasions. Administrators should be allowed to "drop in" and see the real, everyday teacher at work. This way all teachers would be on their toes, and the teaching profession would be rid of those who are truly not dedicated. Children are the real losers when poor teachers go undetected.

All the topics discussed in this chapter take time to work out. You will find by the end of the first year you will make many changes in how you plan and teach various subjects. As a teacher, you never stop learning or growing in your ability to develop lessons and come up with better methods to teach concepts. Scheduling can be a pain, but once you get it down, you are set to work on other aspects of teaching.

2/ Room Arrangement, Management, and Housekeeping

ONCE you have walked into your room and realized that it is yours to set up as you wish, you will probably wonder where to begin. This is an area that is overlooked in college courses, but very important for any teacher before school starts. Time spent here allows you to become better organized and neater.

As soon as you can get into your room, do so! You have no idea how the room was left at the end of the school year. Was it cleaned out, or is there a lot of clutter? Many new teachers wait until too late and then find they have no time to clean out closets and shelves, and set them up in a way that will work best for them.

One of the first things you should do is to go through closets and shelves, which allows you to clean out and rearrange supplies, books, and games. Many times, new teachers find, a lot of general sorting out and throwing away needs to be done, especially if the room belonged to a teacher who was in there for several years (and was a pack rat). Throw away things that have missing pieces, are ripped, or are just plain old and outdated. I suggest putting things in some type of order that makes sense to you. Try to put things together (for example, math books, workbooks, games, manipulatives), so everything is in one general area. Keep art supplies together, arrange construction paper by color and size, and place these near the sink. This way students will be able to get supplies without bothering you, and will be near a sink for easy clean-up. Put bulletin board supplies together and label them so you can get what you need without looking for it. Playground equipment and games should be placed where students can get them easily. This enables them to assume responsibility for keeping those areas tidy. Materials you are going to be using frequently should be placed near your desk. Higher shelves should house those things you do not wish to have for student use.

The reason for doing all this is to make it easier throughout the year to find things. You really don't have a lot of extra minutes to waste, looking for things you know you have . . . somewhere! Doing this before school begins lets you know what you have to work with and what items you may need to buy. Some districts allow money in the budget for new teachers to purchase some supplies and materials. Also, check to see if all audio-visual equipment in your room is in good working condition. There is nothing worse than getting ready to use a projector, only to find it doesn't work. Believe me, the time spent doing the things discussed above may seem monotonous and irrelevant, but when it is done you will save yourself much time and many headaches. You will know where things are, and find it easier to inventory when the time comes to do so.

Room Arrangement

Once you have had the opportunity to clean out and reorganize closets and shelves, concentrate on setting up your room. Determine where you will be doing most of your whole class teaching and which blackboard you will use. You should arrange students' desks within this area before arranging any other furniture. All students should have a clear view of the board, and should not be sitting with their backs to you. Keep in mind that windows are very distracting, so try not to place desks near them. Sit in various desks to get a viewpoint from their perspective.

Most teachers begin with rows until they have had the opportunity to establish control, and to find out their students' personalities. By October I begin to use different arrangements. I start students in groups of two and work up to groups of six. I do not believe in all-boy or all-girl groupings, because then you have segregated groups. Boys and girls need to interact with each other and build friendships. I like to put desks in different formations (a U-shape and circle are good ones to try), because it creates more space in the room. I do a lot of teaching having students meet in a circle at the back of the room. All students are then arranged so they are on an equal basis, and eye contact can be made with all members of the group. No desks are in the way, so distractions are very minimal. I find students pay attention better, and are more apt to share information if I am "part of the group." Teachers who stand in front of the room to do their teaching are often seen as domineering by the students. However, you may have some years where you cannot deviate from individual rows, due to the type of students you have. As I have said many times throughout this guide, work with what is best suited to your individual teaching style and the students you have in your class.

Once you have placed student desks, figure out where you should place your own desk. Depending on your preference, you may choose to place your desk at the front, side, or back of the room. Some teachers like the front, because they can see everything that is going on, and remain where they can be in total control. Others like the back, because students cannot see or be distracted by what is going on at the teacher's desk. I prefer to be at the side, near the front, where I can see students' faces and establish eye contact with them. I find it easier to observe them in this position without them thinking I am staring at them. I feel I still maintain control of the classroom, but not in a dominating way.

I also like to make sure my desk is near a bookcase, or shelves where I can store papers, books, and Teacher's Manuals. I cannot function with a desk that is cluttered and messy. Storing things elsewhere alleviates this. Students, even though they are not allowed to touch things on your desk, love to come up and look over what is there, as if they might find it contains something terrific. I also like to place my desk so students cannot get behind it. I do not like people looking over my shoulder when I am trying to work. Make sure that wherever you place your desk, you have a clear view of every area in the room. You must be able to see students at all times.

The last couple of things to place are any tables, and a file cabinet if you are lucky enough to have one. If you are going to be using your file cabinet a lot, then put it by your desk for easy filing. Some teachers use it as a divider, or place it by the door. Placing it by the door allows you to store lunch, attendance, and dismissal slips, plus bus passes for easy reference. When you are figuring out where to put your table(s), determine what you will be using each one for (e.g., meeting with groups, doing projects, or displaying things). Then you can put them in spots where you think these purposes would be best served. If you are using a table to meet with groups, make sure your chair is positioned where you can see your whole class. I like to place tables at the back and side of the room where students will not be disturbed if they are working at their seats. I also try to save a corner of the room large enough for students to meet together in a circle formation. To give you a basic feel of how rooms can be set up, I have diagrammed two different ways in Figure 2.1 (see pages 16–17). It is best to change your room at least four times during the school year. This way students do not become bored by their surroundings, and it helps them adjust better to change.

Make sure you allow space for students to store belongings that will not fit into their desks (e.g., lunch boxes, coats, footwear, backpacks, show and tell items). Many rooms are equipped with closets or lockers within the room itself, or in the hallway. Students should be made aware that it is their responsibility to keep these areas clean and tidy.

When you have set up your room, look over the following list, which includes important things to consider in any room arrangement. After you have read the list, refer to the two diagrams (Figure 2.1) to see how these things have been taken into account.

- When placing desks, try to be sure students have enough space to move without bothering other students.
- Look over the general setup of the room. Does it allow for traffic to move smoothly without interruption of students? Are high-traffic areas free of congestion?
- Does the setup make the room look cluttered or crowded? Does it look like a comfortable room the students will enjoy being in?
- Is there easy access to the sink, bathroom, fire window, and door?
- Are busy spots away from areas where concentration is needed?
- Can students see all display areas, blackboard(s), the movie screen?
- Can you see all students clearly?
- Are electrical outlets accessible?

Before school begins there are some pieces of equipment you need to make sure your room contains. The following list contains items you will definitely use, either daily or at special times throughout the year. Making sure your room is well supplied with these things saves unnecessary trips to the nurse's office and cafeteria.

- tissues
- first aid kit or bandaids (see your school nurse)

- plastic gloves (see your school nurse)
- paper towels (see your custodian)
- soap (see your custodian)
- plastic spoons and forks
- paper cups and plates
- napkins and straws (see the cafeteria staff)
- juice opener
- teacher's bell
- timer (optional)

Odds and Ends

Other classroom management concerns teachers often forget until the first day of school are the items listed below. It is much better to know how you will handle these situations before they come up in the classroom. By being prepared, you will not need to make snap decisions concerning important aspects of classroom management.

(1) What type of heading will students use on their papers? Make sure you either have an example displayed on poster paper, or on the blackboard for at least the first month of school.

(2) What is the bottom line on neatness of papers that you will accept? Will students be made to re-do the paper(s)? If so, when?

(3) Are class rules and consequences posted and displayed where they can be seen easily by students? (If you decide to include the class with organizational rules, then just be sure to save room to post a copy.)

(4) How will you handle students who are absent and must make up work?

(5) Select an area on the board where daily assignments and due dates will be posted. This should not change locations.

(6) Due dates must be given with assignments. How will you handle students who either do not turn in assignments, or are late with them?

(7) Make sure that when you give directions for assignments, you also put them on the board. Questioning a few students will help you in asssessing whether directions were clear and understand-

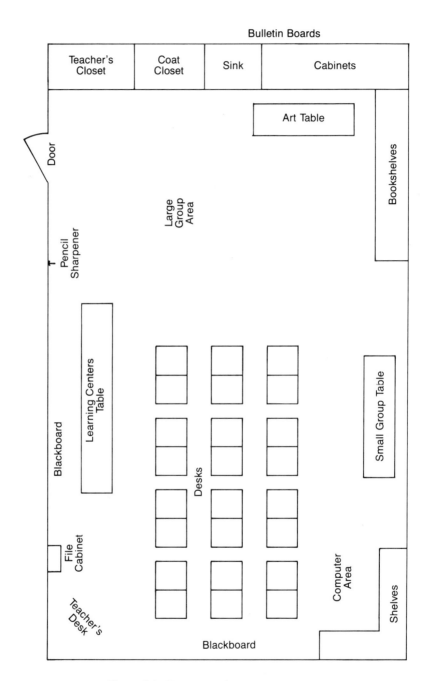

Figure 2.1 *Two types of room arrangements.*

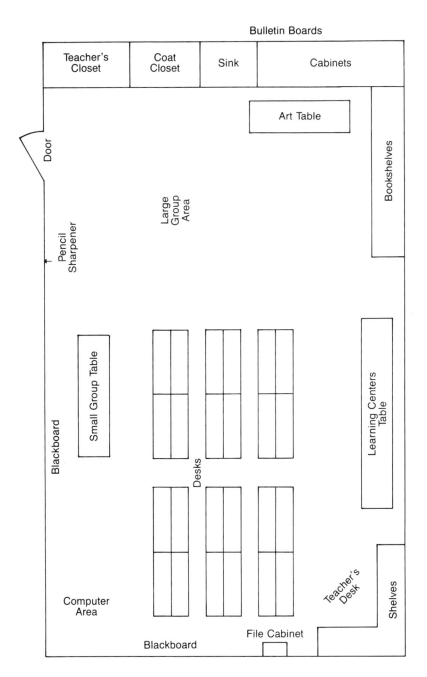

Figure 2.1 (continued) *Two types of room arrangements.*

able. Allow students to ask questions before beginning any assignment.

Make sure you have a copy of students' phone numbers and their parent's names at home. I always save the first page of my plan book to record this in, plus birthdays, addresses, and ages of brothers and sisters. I take my plan book home on a nightly basis, so I find this is a good place for vital information to be kept should I need it outside of school.

Involving Students in Housekeeping

Since I am a person who must have a neat and tidy room to work in, I cannot tolerate other teachers' rooms that are messy. Teachers who say they are too busy "teaching" and have no time to keep up with housekeeping duties are missing the opportunity to let students assume this responsibility. Students love to clean, and can be taught to pick up after themselves. At the end of the day allow students to pick up papers from the floor, wash countertops and blackboards, dust, and arrange desks neatly.

Many teachers choose students to be classroom helpers. Once a week they change students' jobs, always on a rotating basis so everyone gets a new job. Suggestions for jobs include: dusting; washing blackboards; cleaning countertops; straightening coat closets; serving as messenger, line leader, or paper passer; taking lunch count and attendance; cleaning up the lunch room; watering plants; sweeping the floor; changing the calendar; keeping the schedule; emptying trash cans, putting chairs up at the end of the day. You may think of other jobs in your room that would be suitable for students to do.

It takes me about a month to show my third graders how to do the housekeeping chores, but in the long run it saves me a lot of time. They love to keep the room clean, and they watch out to ensure that other students pick up after themselves. The janitor once told me she loved to clean my room, because there wasn't much to do. It always looked neat.

Students need to learn that school is not just a place where academics are stressed, but that responsibility to self and others is an important part of the schooling process. Remember that students love to help; let them do so and your job becomes easier. If you act as a role model and truly care about the way the classroom looks, students will care too. I love it when students tell me I have a neat desk, because it shows that I am sending the message that not only do I expect them to be neat, I am, too.

Room Time Savers

Keeping things neat in your room is made easier when you utilize plastic baskets and crates for storing things. These come in a variety of sizes and colors and can be moved easily to clean under. The colors help to spruce up the classroom and add a decorative touch. I like to put the crates on their sides and place a board on the top where I can put flowers. Flowers help make the classroom look alive. If you choose to use bookends on top, buy the kind with cork on the bottom as the other kind are always falling over.

In most schools, teachers are required to save bus passes, permission slips, and absentee excuses, and to turn them in at the end of the school year. I use two large paper clips — one for bus passes and the other for absentee slips, so when students give me one, it goes to the back of the pile. At the end of the month I put a rubber band around each stack, label the stacks by month, and put them in two large manila envelopes. If a problem arises and I need to find one of them, it will be fairly easy to locate. Make sure at the beginning of the year that you find out exactly which hand-in slips you need to keep. Do not throw away anything without first checking, as you may need it for documentation later on. I even save every note that parents send in, and clip them together. You never know when they may come in handy. There is more on this subject in the "Record Keeping, Documentation, and Pupil Files" chapter.

I am always amazed at how much mail I receive at school. Do not let it pile up on you; eliminate the junk mail. The first year I kept a folder in my file cabinet labeled "Educational Merchandise" but have found a magazine holder works even better. I put in it any catalogs, advertisements, and brochures, that contain merchandise I might be interested in ordering in the spring. That way, when it comes time in the spring to order for the next school year, everything is in one place. I also keep any information that should be kept as a reference in a folder for future use.

I always run off a few extra dittos in case some do not come out clearly. At the end of each week, I put all the extra ones in a basket for students to use as scrap paper or take home for extra practice.

Keeping your room organized, and keeping materials so that both students and you know where to find them, will keep your room looking clean and neat. Your job at the end of the school year will be much smoother if you keep up with things. Administrators tell me they do not enjoy observing in rooms that look cluttered and unorganized. How your room looks is one criterion on which you are evaluated in many school districts. Colleges often forget to stress the importance of the contents discussed in this chapter. Teaching covers so much more than just presenting lessons to students. How your room is arranged, managed and kept on a daily basis is a reflection of how prepared you are in the total teaching picture. The biggest tips to remember include:

- Let students help keep the room clean and neat.
- Do not let things accumulate.
- Arrange the room in a manner that accents your particular teaching style.
- Don't put off until tomorrow what you can do today!

3/⁄⁄⁄ Discipline

DISCIPLINE problems are by far one of the hardest areas for teachers to handle, no matter how many years they have taught. It seems that once you counteract one problem, another one comes along. Children today are faced with a multitude of problems unheard of decades ago. Ask any school psychologist or counselor about their schedules, and they will tell you that their days are overflowing with problems that are emotional, social, or behavioral in nature. A child who is a discipline problem is a child with problems!

Discipline problems create real headaches for teachers because they divert energy away from teaching. In most cases, discipline problems must be faced immediately, and therefore they take learning time from those students who do behave. Students who consistently misbehave wear a teacher down to feelings of inadequacy and helplessness.

What can you do? You may find some help from the principal, counselor, or psychologist, but even if you do you will inevitably be forced to assume the brunt of the situation yourself. This chapter is not designed to give you any instant solutions, but will review some of the more popular methods, and will give you some suggestions and ideas that have worked for fellow teachers.

Preventing Discipline Problems

Maintaining effective classroom management requires learning different techniques that help sustain an environment suitable for learning. Jacob Kounin has developed five techniques to help minimize misbehavior: with-it-ness, overlapping, smoothness, momentum, and group alerting.

(1) With-it-ness exists when teachers are aware of everything that is going on in the classroom. If you are giving a lecture, and a student starts talking to a neighbor, you would simply go over and stand by that student, but continue speaking. Anyone who is off-task is drawn back into the mainstream of whatever is happening. You let students know you are aware of what they are doing by demonstrating with-it-ness behavior.

(2) Overlapping occurs when you attend to two events at the same time. An example of this would be if a student comes to you for help when you are working with a small group, and you are able to maintain control of both situations.

(3) Another technique is smoothness, which means that you stay on the topic at hand—you do not stray off on tangents. You don't begin a lesson, and then ask if everyone has signed up for lunch. Once students have begun work, you do not interrupt them for anything.

(4) Momentum occurs when you keep a lesson moving at a good pace. You do not elaborate on things that students already know.

(5) The last technique is called group alerting, meaning keeping students on their toes, or in suspense. They do not know when you are going to call on them, so they listen attentively, anticipating your questioning them. If you ask a child to demonstrate something at the blackboard, you also ask students at their seats to do something.

Using these five methods allows you as a teacher to maintain control of your classroom, without stopping and starting, as you deal with problems that arise and look for students who are not active participants.

General Tips

Before you meet your class, you must already have in mind what type of discipline action and consequences you will use. How will you deal with misbehaving students, homework, fighting, or cheating? It is fine to allow students to help come up with rules, but you must have a say in formulating them. You should not have any more than five rules, because then there are too many to follow. Tying rules into categories (e.g., No hitting, punching, biting, kicking could be lumped together as— "No Hurting Others") will help you stay within five. Post the rules in a highly conspicuous place. I send a copy of rules home so parents know what they are and can discuss them with their children.

Students must know from day one what to expect. Do not let them find loopholes so they can get away with something. In class meetings the first couple of weeks I use students to role play various discipline problems that could come up. We discuss the feelings of those involved, how a given problem affects others, and we find solutions. The biggest thing to remember is to be consistent and fair! Students are going to push you the first month to see what they can and cannot get away with. You must follow through. If you say you are going to do something—DO IT! Many times I've seen teachers pushed to their limits, and they make a threat that they either can't, or are unprepared to follow through on. Don't let this happen to you, or you could be in for a long, hard, year!

You can be firm but friendly at the same time. Most new teachers seem to be concerned that their students won't like them, which interferes with the discipline process. Believe me, if you run a fair classroom, care about your students, make school interesting and challenging, students will respect you and discipline problems will not be as serious. I let students know from day one that I honestly care about them. I demonstrate this by listening to what they say and giving lots of hugs and warm fuzzies! If you develop a good rapport with students, I strongly feel they are not going to misbehave, because they will want your respect and do not want to hurt your feelings. I have never had serious discipline problems because I expect respect from students. They will live up to your expectations. I find that instead of yelling at students, taking time to talk to them does more. I also let students get to know me on a personal level, and based on my experiences, find this cuts down on misbehavior.

I had a child in my room who came from an abusive home and therefore learned early in life that in order to get attention, he must misbehave. The first couple of weeks he tried everything to get attention. He was mean and antagonized his classmates. I saw it was quickly becoming the class versus the child.

To alleviate the problem, I sent the child on an errand during a class meeting, and discussed with the rest of the class his situation. We had to teach him, by showing him how to get along with others and how to behave properly. I told the class that the room could never be a happy and enjoyable place if there was tension between any members, that we must be together for a year and must make the best of the situation. I tried to show them that we are like a family and must talk about any problems openly, so everyone can function to the best of their ability. When the child returned, we included him in the discussion, and told him we were going to be his friends, no matter what he tried. Suggestions were given to him on how to be a friend, and when he felt he had to act out, he should go to the thinking chair to calm down.

Eventually, the child's negative behavior decreased, and he began to open up and blossom. It took time, and sometimes I found it extremely hard not to become angry with him. I counted to ten many times and prayed for patience! I have often wondered how that child was doing, as he moved the next year and I did not see him again. He is an example of a child searching for love and learning to give it in a positive way. As I said before, I find that discussing things works more than any other method.

A quick look at the market shows many books that claim to solve discipline problems. If it were that easy, why are such a variety of books constantly being written? Many education discipline classes have waiting lists and are constantly filled. What works for one child may not work for others, which is why teachers must be familiar with different techniques.

Discipline Models

Assertive Discipline

One of the best selling books on the market, *Assertive Discipline*, written by Lee and Marlene Canter, is a systematic approach. It is designed to promote a teacher's rights by focusing on the right to teach without extreme interruptions or minimal distractions. Teachers usually respond to conflicts in one of three ways: nonassertively, hostilely, or assertively. It is the assertive teacher who develops specific rules, a reward system for positive behavior, and consequences for negative behavior. The discipline plan is based on the teacher's desires and the limits of tolerance toward student behaviors, and therefore the teacher does not back down when dealing with misbehavior. Each teacher writes a plan, shares it with the principal for approval, and has each parent and student sign it.

Students who violate rules are dealt with quickly and directly, allowing teachers to have maximum control in this approach. Students are held accountable for proper behavior in the classroom, and are not to question why. They know what is expected of them. Assertive discipline advocates feel that teachers can influence students' behavior and reduce the frequency of problem behavior by rewarding students who follow the rules with positive incentives. This approach gives the teacher the upper hand in the situation, and leaves no room for negotiation. Rules are clear and consistent, and the consequences used are effective deterrents. Teachers do not have to deal with problems by themselves, as they have established support with the principal and parents.

Moral Development

Moral development is another approach to discipline. This approach also maintains that control must be established, but with an eye to the long-range development of the student's moral character. Moral growth is a developmental process occurring in stages, starting at birth and continuing through adulthood. Teachers aware of this growth, and what is normal for each stage, can raise the moral reasoning level of their students. The moral development approach stresses cooperative learning as a way of fostering positive peer relations, self-esteem, and a good classroom community. When teachers and students work together in setting up rules and discussing their purpose, students are more apt to behave because they understand the values behind the rules. They will begin to respect themselves and others, both inside and outside the classroom. Moral reasoning, self-control, and respect for teachers can be developed along with voluntary compliance to rules, and responsibility to self and the group as a moral community.

The moral development approach asserts that teachers must be effective and competent in the instructional process, well-organized, and aware of what is happening in the classroom before moral development can take place. The teacher is the central figure in the classroom, but he/she values the student's opinion and feels the students are mature enough to handle responsibility. One of the most important points is for teachers to respect their students, and require respect in return. Teachers must practice what they preach, teach through examples, and be willing to guide, listen, and advise to help students develop a positive self-concept and an understanding of right and wrong. The long-range goal is for students to learn how to think for themselves and to appreciate the perspectives of others.

One strength of moral development is that it moves students away from a dependence on external controls and toward internal control. Individual conferences are held with students who repeatedly misbehave to solve the problem, thus helping them to take responsibility for improving their behavior. The key strength is the cooperation and mutual respect between teachers and students and the emphasis on developing a community feeling in the classroom. The moral development approach to discipline is explained in detail in Thomas Lickona's book, *Educating for Character* (Bantam, 1991).

T.E.T.

The third method is called T.E.T.: Teacher Effectiveness Training. This approach was devised by Thomas Gordon. It is based on the theory made popular by Carl Rogers, which suggests that all of a child's experiences will determine what he or she becomes. Given empathic understanding, warmth, and openness, a child will choose what is best for himself or herself and become a constructive and trustworthy person. The child is seen as rational and when misbehavior occurs, it is a result of this natural rationality being stifled. This would occur in classrooms where teachers order, direct, or force students to behave according to "their" will.

Teachers who use T.E.T. listen carefully to the student's statements, appear interested, and show understanding by mirroring the student's feelings and perceptions. The teacher's role is strictly noncritical and totally trusts in the child's ability to identify and solve problems. The students, by being encouraged to express their feelings and ideas, will come to the root of the problem and trust their own capabilities, as they explore and expand upon ways to solve the problem. The way students solve these problems is directly related to their self-concept, how they see themselves—either as competent or incompetent in meeting challenges. By dealing with daily problems they control their own destinies. This model gives ownership of the problem to the students, who in turn must deal with it. Teachers must be trained in this technique and often find it very time-consuming to implement.

Reality Discipline

The reality discipline approach, developed by William Glasser, believes that people must be helped to acknowledge their behavior as irresponsible, and then take action to make it productive and logical. Everyone must satisfy their own needs without infringing on someone else's. Misbehavior results from the failure of schools and teachers to fulfill needs. Students want to learn and experience success, to feel self-worthy, but they are hindered by things like grades, teacher lectures, irrelevant subject matter, and the lack of sufficient discussions and experiments. Students placed in classrooms like these are bored, unhappy, and find things irrelevant.

Children must learn to identify behavior that hurts them, or others, and then make plans to solve the problem. Children who do so will become responsible for their own behavior and learn self-control. When students break a rule, they are asked the following questions: What are you doing? Why? Is it helping you? Is it against the rules? What will you do to change that? Consistency is the key to making it work. The teacher accepts no excuses, repeats the questions stated above again, and then makes students go to a time-out place to develop a plan to stop the behavior from occurring again. (A time-out place is a certain spot where students go in the classroom to be alone, and contains no stimuli. Students go there to think and regain control of positive behavior.) The plan includes steps for following it, and consequences for failing to meet it. The teacher may have input on the plan, but it is mostly written by the student. After each plan is written and implemented, the teacher and student meet to evaluate whether it is working. Parental support is a must and discipline will not be effective if there is no support from home.

Class Meetings

To aid in the success of the reality discipline approach, classroom meetings are a must. If you are unfamiliar with these, they are held in a circle at a specific time, anywhere from 10–30 minutes with young children and 30–45 with older children. They are led by the teacher or student, and everyone is encouraged to share, as there are no "wrong" answers. The teacher and students express their ideas, opinions, and feelings on a variety of topics.

Classroom meetings raise self-esteem, foster communication and problem solving, and increase moral reasoning, leadership, and listening skills. There are three types of meetings Glasser speaks of that you should become familiar with: open-ended, educational/diagnostic, and problem solving. Open-ended meetings are ones in which students create their own fantasies and explore imaginary problems. The educational/diagnostic meeting is one where a topic being studied by the students is discussed to see what they know and don't know, and to determine further interest. The teacher can then use that information to make decisions about what would be essential to cover and what would be most relevant. The last type of meeting is problem solving, where the class focuses on a real problem and offers solutions. (This may include problems of fellow classmates.)

I use classroom meetings and urge you to try them. Since I have initiated them I find my class a much more caring and democratic community. There is definitely a sense of shared responsibility and increased participation among all. Don't try meetings once and give up. Most students have not been involved in such a setup and need time to open up and share their feelings, without feeling threatened.

At the first meeting you should establish rules. I have the group set them up because they are more apt to respect and follow them when they have a say in the formation. My students usually come up with rules such as: raise hands, but only after the person is done speaking (otherwise the speaker feels rushed); no talking or negative comments; and stay on the subject being discussed. Rules should be simple, and there should be no more than five; otherwise, there will be too many for students to remember.

The teacher's role is to make sure rules are followed. He/she must help develop listening and speaking skills, and encourage students to participate and react to the opinions of others. Good opening and follow-up questions must also be prepared to stimulate active thinking and discussion. The teacher must finally bring the meeting to a close. The Reality Discipline approach, with students accepting responsibility for their actions and becoming involved in class meetings, helps

Behavior Modification

The behavior modification movement was led by B. F. Skinner, who believed students behave because adults have rewarded correct behavior and ignored or punished irrational behavior. Therefore, misbehavior may be changed and reshaped by changing the student's environment. If a teacher wants a child to behave in a certain manner, he/she must control the child's environment. This approach doesn't believe in discussing a child's "inner feelings" or expecting a child to come up with a solution. The teacher must come up with positive reinforcers to help the student behave appropriately. Three types of positive reinforcers include: token reinforcement, social reinforcement, and primary reinforcement. Token reinforcers are items given to students after desired behavior is shown and can be traded in for materials, special privileges, or reinforcing events. Social reinforcers are things like: smiles, nods, gestures, praise, attention, and approval after the desired result is achieved. Examples of primary reinforcers include sweets, popcorn, or cereal, which satisfy biological needs. For the student who misbehaves, negative reinforcers (e.g., those things that a student does not desire) are used. Punishment is not to be confused with negative reinforcers because although punishment may stop the behavior, it does not show the child what is expected of him or her.

Behavior modification is more scientifically controlled and validated than the other approaches. If the teacher wants to stop a behavior, she/he must count how many times the behavior occurs in a certain amount of time, which is called the baseline measure. The next step is to use reinforcers over a specific time period. When this period is up, the teacher notes how many times the behavior now occurs and charts it to make a comparison. The third step is called reversal, in which the reinforcement is taken away and a new score is taken and plotted on the chart. If the score rises dramatically, the reinforcers are having an effect and the teacher can go back to using them. Over a period of time the reinforcers should be gradually withdrawn and a postcheck score taken to see if behavior is lasting and has a long-term effect.

Teachers must be aware not to use negative reinforcement such as raised eyebrows, scowls, frowns, or staring, with a child they are trying to reshape because they may actually be reinforcing the behavior. By ignoring incorrect behavior and concentrating on correct behavior, the teacher is using extinction. As a result, the child will probably increase negative behavior, but if the teacher can stick it out through this period, the child eventually realizes it is useless and decreases the behavior. This is particularly tough on teachers, but it is important during this time to reward any positive behavior. A teacher has to behave in the same manner that he/she desires from their students. One problem with this approach is that while you are working with the student who is acting up, how do you keep the rest of the class under control?

Some guidelines to remember when using reinforcers are to reward frequently and immediately after the correct behavior occurs, and to break behavior into small steps and reward them (don't start too big). Set up the behavior plan with students so they know what they must do to get rewarded. This is also referred to as contingency contracting. The key is to give the child a sense of accomplishment and satisfaction.

There are two types of schedules that can be used when setting up the contingency contracts—fixed interval and ratio interval. Fixed interval is usually used first, where the child receives a token every time a desired behavior occurs. Ratio interval is where a child is rewarded periodically but doesn't know when. A combination of schedules can also be used.

A time-out area is also used, but this is a place where a student goes to get away from the reinforcing situation. The area must not be reinforcing, and isolation from any type of stimuli is a must in order to be effective.

Saturation is another type of intervention used. Saturation is a forced repetition of the negative behavior until it becomes tiring and then it serves as a negative reinforcer.

This approach stresses positive behavior, but can be very time-consuming, especially if you have several students with whom you need to plan. I find behavior modification is very successful with those children who come from unfavorable home situations and misbehave to get attention. Many of the teachers I interviewed used positive and negative reinforcers in their classrooms even though they do not follow this approach 100 percent.

Social Discipline

The last of the discipline models I will discuss is the social discipline model of Rudolf Dreikurs. He believes that all people need to belong and be accepted by others. Misbehavior, as he sees it, is a result of children trying to fill that inner need by acting in an annoying, destructive, or hostile manner that they believe will gain them acceptance in their peer group.

According to Dreikurs, there are four subconscious goals that motivate misbehavior: attention-getting, power and control, revenge, and helplessness. Attention-getting students are constantly trying to gain attention. Power and control refers to those students who feel inferior, who want to be the boss or get their own way, who force themselves onto others, or who are always bragging and clowning around. A student who cannot get attention or power resorts to "revenge" tactics, often at the expense of others. The last and hardest to help is the student who has given up trying to gain acceptance and doesn't care what happens (helplessness). Adults must intervene and redirect these misplaced goals of children.

The teacher begins to implement this model first by observing and collecting information about the student. This will help the teacher as he/she tries to figure out what goals discussed previously are motivating the student to misbehave.

Once this goal is verified, the teacher helps the student, through the use of directive statements, to learn how to have his or her needs met in socially acceptable ways.

Since the theory stipulates that students are misbehaving to gain acceptance, it recommends that a group effort to discuss such problems be included. Dreikurs believes that students need to practice democratic procedures in school so that they may function in society later. Class meetings or "councils," as this approach calls them, are used to learn such procedures. Decisions are made by the consensus of all members.

The social discipline model does not believe in using positive and negative reinforcement or praise. Natural/logical consequences and encouragement are used instead. A natural consequence refers to what happens as a result of one's behavior. A logical consequence is arranged and related directly to the preceding behavior. If a student is fooling around during reading, the student would be asked to leave and may not return until he/she can be part of the group without bothering anyone. In the meantime, the student may stay in at recess to do the work because he/she won't be bothering anyone at that time. Encouragement is used simultaneously through emphasizing improvement, criticizing only the student's actions, and not allowing the student to compete against others. Praise is not used because the student becomes dependent on the teacher, and when the praise is removed the student returns to old habits. By using encouragement, an environment of accepting the student as worthwhile is created. The key point of this approach is to get the child to be accepted and to be part of the group.

I hope this quick overview of discipline methods proves helpful to you as you begin to set up a discipline plan for your classroom. If you would like to learn more about a particular approach, refer to the reference section. As you know by now, each method has positive and negative qualities. An approach that works well with one child may not work with another. What discipline comes down to is finding an approach that works for you, lets you teach without interruptions, and creates a classroom environment suitable for learning. Discipline is hard, and it may take you time to find a technique with which you can work.

When students get to know you on a personal level, based on my experiences, they are less apt to misbehave. I know many teachers who say you should not get emotionally involved with students, as you then become too subjective. I expect that someday I will get hurt by doing this, yet I cannot stop. When you see students all day, five days a week, it is very hard to not become involved.

Guidelines for Setting Up a Discipline Method

Listed as follows are some guidelines to remember and follow as you set up your discipline method.

(1) Be firm and consistent. Know what you want before you meet students. Treat them as you would want to be treated.
(2) Do not wait to discipline a student; do so immediately.
(3) Give students the opportunity to explain.
(4) Don't put students on the defensive. Don't ask what is wrong with you? Why did you do it? When I talk with students, especially

concerning discipline, I meet them at their level. I prefer to speak with them at eye level where we are both "equal."

(5) Follow through on discipline action every time!

(6) Do not be afraid to tell the class how much you care for them and how great they are. If said enough and with sincerity, the class will believe and try harder to keep your respect.

(7) Don't look down on your students, or dictate "I am teacher, you are students," and therefore demand they look up to you.

(8) Don't make deals with students. ("If you do this, I'll do that.") Dealing undermines your authority and the children's respect for you.

(9) Use positive and negative reinforcers very carefully, and at your own discretion depending on the type of situation. If you use them too often, students will become dependent on them, and will not learn to behave for the correct reasons. Positive reinforcers must not be the primary motivational factor, but are to be used as an extra incentive. The main goal is that students learn to respect you, each other, and become responsible for their own actions.

(10) Try to state rules positively instead of negatively.

(11) Be careful not to gang up on one particular child.

(12) If you need to speak to a child concerning a problem, take him/her to a place where you can talk without the whole class listening.

(13) Most important of all—begin each day with a clean, fresh slate.

Positive and Negative Reinforcers

If you decide to use positive and negative reinforcers, and many teachers do occasionally, I have listed below some possible suggestions to get you started.

Positive Reinforcers

- stickers
- stars, smiley faces, checks
- hugs, pats on the back, praise

- food (pizza, popcorn, ice cream parties)
- behavior awards or certificates
- choice to do brain teasers, word searches, crossword puzzles
- free time
- computer time
- grab bag
- games (board, computer, video)
- special privileges
- listening to records or tapes
- pencils
- choice to read magazines
- send positive notes home to parents
- display work on the bulletin board
- throw out the lowest grade
- allow student the opportunity not to do an assignment
- anything that has to do with a student's particular hobby (e.g., baseball cards)

Negative Reinforcers

- isolation, time-out
- loss of free time, recess, trips, special events
- send to another room
- speak to student
- send papers home for parents to sign
- write name on board
- give extra work
- send daily or weekly reports home to parents
- separate from friends, or move seat
- child writes or calls parents about behavior
- move student by teacher's desk
- after-school suspension
- in-school suspension for major infractions
- at-home suspension in rare cases
- anything that would deter a student from repeating inappropriate behavior

I hope you didn't read this chapter hoping to find an instant solution to discipline and problems caused by the lack of it. As a teacher you must look at each method, and use whatever will work for you in your particular situation. One method is not superior to another, and will not work for all children. I know many teachers who are embarrassed to say they have discipline problems. It is too bad that they can't discuss their problems with other teachers, who might be able to offer suggestions. It would be beneficial to teachers if schools would offer support groups once a month allowing teachers to get together and talk about problems. This would alleviate frustration by allowing problems to be openly discussed, and not continue to build up. It would also stop continual discussion of behavior problems in inappropriate places, such as the teachers' room!

In closing, I would like to share my philosophy of discipline with you. Discipline is the ability to teach children self-control, so that they may function in society and within the boundaries imposed on them. Teach them love and respect and trust every day. If they see and hear these things going on around them, it gets to be a habit. Remind them they are special, unique, and that they can do or be anything they choose to. They are somebody, and they control their own destinies in life. I hope you share the same basic philosophy because our youth is our future!

4/////Learning Centers

MANY classrooms today utilize learning centers as an effective way to increase the productivity of students. You will find centers a great way to make sure students are doing something constructive with their time. Misbehavior sometimes occurs when students finish work, are not actively involved in the learning process, or already know the material being introduced. Therefore, properly arranged learning centers will help keep your classroom running smoothly. This chapter will provide you with the rationale and key points that will help you to set up a learning center in your room.

Learning centers can be defined as areas in the classroom with activities and materials that teach, enrich, or reinforce a variety of skills or concepts. Teachers use learning centers to follow up a lesson already taught, for small group instruction, or for individual activities. I have noticed that teachers who incorporate learning centers are able to offer a variety of activities that allow for the overall growth of all their students, no matter what their academic level is. Effective learning centers offer a variety of activities and materials ranging from simple to difficult, and concrete to abstract. They also are geared to the needs, interests, and abilities of students.

The rationale behind the development of learning centers is that children learn best when they are actively involved in learning, and when their developmental level matches the task they are pursuing. Taking into account that children learn at different rates and in a variety of styles, learning centers provide options for these styles and rates. Children who are actively involved assume responsibility for what they are learning, and they are encouraged by an environment that provides raw materials for this to take place.

When you allow students to move from center to center, their spans of attention remain high, in contrast to the attention spans of children who are asked to stay seated for long periods of time. Learning centers keep children interested by allowing them the use of the center for independent study, as a follow-up to a teacher taught, or for enrichment activity. These areas of study are not only a valuable option, but most importantly, because children are actively involved and interested in what they are learning, the amount of misbehavior is drastically reduced.

You may find that learning centers sometimes increase the noise level in your room. When students are excited about what they are doing, and are moving from center to center, they are more apt to be vocal. You will have to work with students in helping them to learn self-control. Your tolerance of noise and activity may have to increase some, but remember it is better to have children turned on to learning because they are excited than turned off because they are bored!

Now that you have a basic understanding of what learning centers are, it is important to establish some guidelines for planning and actually implementing learning centers in your room. First of all, learning centers should not be set up as just a place for students to use when they have finished their work, because students will view them as an extra and not pursue them seriously. Provide a time when all students are using the centers. The purpose of centers is not to keep children busy, but to provide them with valuable learning activities. Be careful not to allow learning centers to degenerate into places where students are not actively learning. It is okay to use dittos for practice on skills, but remember to use other materials such as puzzles, games, and manipulatives to promote learning. Activity-oriented materials are supported by the theory that children learn and retain more by actual hands-on experience.

Record Keeping

For your record keeping you should provide a means for students to account for the time they have spent at the center and the learning that took place. This will give you a basis for determining if students are spending their time wisely, using the centers effectively, and choosing different centers. If you find students are not using a particular center, you will need to re-evaluate its purpose. Is the material inappropriate, boring, or repetitious? Is it too easy, or too hard? Centers should be appealing and attractive, with a variety of activities and/or materials. Ask yourself if this is a place where you would go. If not, chances are that students won't want to go there either.

In kindergarten, record keeping can be very simple. I had a wheel with centers listed on the large circle, and names listed on a smaller circle. Each day I would turn the wheel and students would go to a different center. Parent volunteers would help in each center during this time. Also, at each center I had a large chart with all the activities one could do there listed at the top, students' names were listed at the side. If the student successfully completed the activity, the parent would let her/him choose a sticker and place it on the chart. If it was too difficult the parent would put a check-mark on the chart. If it was not completed, I had the abbreviation, INC. written in. This allowed me to see which activities each student had done, as well as the problem areas he or she was experiencing (see Figure 4.1).

In third grade I used a chart like the one in Figure 4.1, but also had students keep track in their center folder. I had a sheet of paper in the folder, which had the activity, the date, the amount of time spent there, and whether it was completed (see Figure 4.2.). Students filled these in each time they went to a center. I collected five folders daily to keep track of what was happening, and by the end of the week I had gone through each student's folder. I also left room for their comments. They wrote one or two sentences about what they learned at the center on that day.

In a class meeting or through a suggestion box, let students give you some ideas on the development of centers, as this will help them to be involved and interested. Encourage students to develop activities for learning centers, and to add new materials and activities. Seek input from community resources available to you, such as parents, other teachers, administrators, colleagues, and senior citizens; these are tremendous, usually untapped resources. Regularly change the activities and materials in the centers; fresh ideas will appeal more than stale ones!

Integrating Centers

Tie centers into one another and into other classroom activities so that carry-over can be made into the other subjects you are teaching.

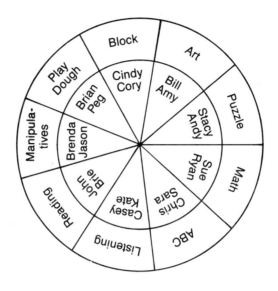

ABC Center

	Matching	UpperCase Sounds	ABC Puzzle
Amy	★	Inc.	
Bill	★	✓	
John	★	★	★
Jane	★	★	Inc.
Casey	✓		
Kate	Inc.		
Jason	★	★	✓

Figure 4.1 *Learning center record keeping for whole class.*

Center	Activity	Date	Amount of Time	Completed	Comments
English	ABC Order	1/3	15 Minutes	Yes	I learned you must go to the 3rd letter to alphabetize.

Figure 4.2 Individualized record keeping.

For example, when my third grade students began studying nutrition, I developed activities in the different centers around the theme of nutrition. The Science Center included different experiments (testing for fat, protein, sugar). In the Math Center a grocery store with empty cartons and boxes, provided students with the chance to go shopping and to pay for their purchases with play money. Language Arts had students looking up and defining words such as vitamins, materials, protein, and starch, and listing the appropriate food under each heading. Learning to read labels also fitted into this center. In the Art Center students made collages of the food groups, and designed their own food product complete with their own advertisement. In the Social Studies Center students did research on what countries produced which food. Tying centers into one another provided students with a unique way to learn about nutrition. Students were eager to develop and bring in materials for all the centers.

Each center must not only be labeled, but must also tell how many students may use the center at one time. This will cut down on overcrowding. Introduce what the purpose of each center is, what can be done there, and what materials, games, and activities are available, so students are clear on what is expected of them. Lay the ground rules and the consequences for breaking these rules, and make sure you consistently enforce them. This is essential to the effectiveness of centers in your room. Clear, consistent rules are a must! Make sure students know how to pick up the center when they are finished. Remember, some students have never had the opportunity to use learning centers. For the first few weeks, assigning students to centers and activities will help with the transition. Eventually, you will be able to offer more choices and let students choose the centers they wish to.

Center Checklist

I find the checklist outlined below very helpful as I develop a learning center from the initial stages to the actual implementation. It was given to me in one of my education courses, but I cannot find any reference to anyone who developed it. It basically covers everything discussed so far, in regards to developing a learning center. You will find it much easier to glance at this list than to reread the beginning of the chapter. For my own personal use, I find it best to make up several copies of this checklist. As I develop each center I write in what applies under the appropriate heading.

 I. Objectives
  A. Central purpose for the center
  B. Specific purpose for each level, activity or content area
 II. Tools and Materials
 III. Operational Procedures
  A. Introduction of center to students
  B. General directions for the use of the center
  C. Well-defined procedures—directions to student for each
   activity
 IV. Provision for Evaluation—this may be built in as part of
  the operational procedure.

As you begin to plan for the arrangement of centers in your room, you must take into consideration two things—movable and immovable fixtures. First, draw a blueprint of the room. Include everything that is not movable, such as built-in shelves, blackboards, closets, windows, doors, and plumbing. This is necessary so that you can plan around these features as you decide where to place each center. Now make a list of everything movable—desks, tables, chairs. These things can be arranged around the centers.

Most teachers who use centers tell me they do all the planning on paper; it is less time-consuming and tiring in regards to moving furniture. Another thing to keep in mind in your planning stages is keeping a smooth flow of traffic. On your blueprint you should plan how students will get from place to place. One entrance to a center works best. Make sure the entrance is big enough to allow children to move in and out without interfering with the dynamics of that center.

The most important thing to keep in mind is to make sure the quiet and noisy centers are placed far apart. You cannot set up an art center or block center next to a language arts center where students are trying to read and write. Figure 4.3 shows a possible setup for a nursery or kindergarten room. This is basically how my room was set up when I taught three- to six-year-olds. I arranged the room several ways, but this setup worked best not only for my students, but for me.

Each center included the following items:

(1) Blocks—all blocks, cars, trucks
(2) Art—playdough, easel, paint, fingerpaint, paper, scissors, clay, chalk, crayons
(3) Large motor—climbing equipment
(4) Dramatics or Housekeeping—dress-up clothes, play stove, sink, refrigerator, dolls, crib, pots and pans
(5) Meeting area
(6) Manipulatives—puzzles, games, beads
(7) Math—games, flashcards, shapes, numbers
(8) Language Arts
   • Reading—all books (reference, picture, text)
   • Writing—paper, pencils, pictures, chalkboards, typewriter, chalkboard
   • Listening—record player, tape player, tapes, records, headphones
(9) Science—aquarium, animals, magnets, magnifying glasses, sand, water play, plants, microscope

If you take a closer look at the diagram, you will notice that I tried to set up the room so that students who are in the noisy areas are not directly facing students who are trying to read, write, or use the manipulatives. The noisy areas are far enough away from the quiet ones so they do not interfere with each other. The art and science areas are right next to the sink so that students do not have to walk through other areas to wash hands. It is imperative that all materials and supplies be kept in the areas in which they are used. Students should not need to interrupt other areas to get supplies.

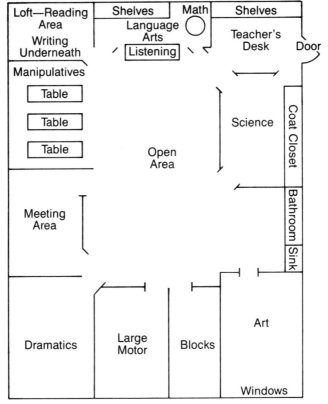

Figure 4.3 *Center arrangement for kindergarten or nursery school room.*

You will find that you have to keep rearranging your setup of centers until you get something that works for you and your students. What works one year may not work the next with a new group of students. You may have to combine or delete centers if you do not have a lot of space in your room. For example, the science and cooking center could be combined. Language arts could be condensed into a smaller space. The types of centers will vary again depending on the grade level you teach.

This introduction to learning centers has been kept brief; for a more detailed look, reference books are included in the resource section. I hope you find learning centers as important to the educational learning process in your room as I do in mine. I have many students who do not want to miss school because of what they will miss during center time. Learning centers take time to work out, but after seven years, I feel very comfortable in setting them up and justifying them to any administrator who may question their effectiveness. Remember to go slowly; if you only have time to set up a few centers, pick the most important ones. Many new teachers start out with language arts and math, and add centers over the years. It is better to create a few good centers that are effective and will give you a positive feeling toward their use, rather than starting with too many, leading to a negative feeling.

5 / Bulletin Boards

THIS chapter will deal with bulletin boards and how to keep them current and relevant, without spending a lot of time and effort on them. Included are tips on creating a bulletin board, plus a few observations on effective and ineffective usage.

One of the first things you notice after you walk into your classroom is how many bulletin boards there are. Many teachers interviewed told me they were afraid they would spend that first year trying to think up ideas, and would barely get one up before it would be time to take another one down. The biggest tip these teachers gave me was to allow students to help with bulletin boards—let them help plan, gather, and cut out material. I wish someone had told me that during my first years of teaching; I would have saved myself a lot of time. I didn't want students to help because I wanted everything perfect in every way. What would administrators and parents think if my bulletin boards were sloppy, letters not even, and things not straight?

As a result, I had beautiful bulletin boards which were all teacher-made and totally ineffective, because students had no input in formulating them. My students couldn't have cared less about the bulletin boards. The longer I taught, the more I began to relax, and I slowly began to let the students help me. By the time I hit public school I decided I had so many other things to learn that bulletin boards would be shared among the students. The school where I teach has large bulletin boards in the halls, which are shared among grade levels. When in October it was my turn to create the bulletin board, I gave all the responsibility to my students. I told them as a group they had to create a theme and prepare the materials to be used. It seemed like Christmas morning; they worked as a group and did a super job. I gave moral support, but they did all the work. I had parents write to me and ask for a picture so they could see the end result. My students couldn't wait to do the next one, and I learned a valuable lesson — students take more interest in and learn more when they are given the opportunity to work together on a general goal. They are also very particular about neatness!

The consensus among teachers was that those containing only materials purchased commercially, those lacking student or teacher input, and those consisting of just pictures, were ineffective bulletin boards. Bulletin boards that look professional yet contain no motivation or participation for students, have no educational value. Bulletin boards that are put up just to fill space, which do not relate to anything being taught, do not represent an effective way to use that area.

Now that you have a general idea of what doesn't work, how do you plan for bulletin boards in your room? Think and look ahead to something coming up in your curriculum that could be a theme for a bulletin board. Think of a sample idea that could be used for the whole month, and then change or add to the idea each year. Save those things you can use again in folders or storage boxes and label these by months. Store cut-out letters in an envelope to be reused again. Some teachers teach only once in their lifetime, because they use the same materials over and over again. Others teach each year beginning with fresh new ideas. Don't save things if your intentions are to never build upon or develop new themes. Take pictures of the good ones to remember the setup, but again, do not put the same ones up year after year! Allow space for a variety of topics — for example, current events or student of the week. Spacing is very important to convey the message and to avoid the "bunching" together of subjects. Bulletin boards should say something; the viewer should be able to see the purpose and develop a quick understanding of what is on display and why. Neatness and clarity should be prevalent; you can teach students how to develop a clear, neat bulletin board that doesn't need to be perfect but on the other hand must not be sloppy.

One of the hardest tasks of the first year is to keep bulletin boards current, relevant, and interesting without spending a lot of time. By planning ahead, tying them into part of your curriculum and working them around a monthly theme, you will save much time. Try to make them part of your learning experience and special to students. Use mostly child-made materials on your bulletin boards by allowing them to display their pictures and stories. The best bulletin boards are those that students help create or those that display their work. A word of caution on displaying students' work: Do not display just the best, but display work of every student.

Select groups of students to develop a bulletin board for each month of the school year. Students really do have creative minds when given the opportunity to express themselves. Try to make sure students work on a month that is especially interesting to them.

I have found that when June comes around, and things begin to wind down, allowing students to cut out figures or shapes for September bulletin boards, is a great way to spend those unplanned moments and a great time saver in August for you. Sometimes I even have students plan and organize bulletin boards, then all I have to do is assemble. I try by the last day of school to have bulletin boards all planned and made so I can store for easy access when it comes August.

Pick a background color that can be used for a few months without replacing it every time you put up a new theme. Use an opaque projector to enlarge ideas and help you develop themes for main bulletin boards. Laminating them will make them durable and allow you to save them for use again. Posters in educational magazines and various book clubs can be laminated and used to develop bulletin boards. Bulletin boards dealing with science kits are an excellent way to expand a concept, such as butterflies, fish, or senses.

The following suggestions for bulletin boards have been used by the teachers I interviewed and found to be especially helpful. One word of caution: When planning bulletin boards, especially at Christmas and Easter, you need to be sensitive to the likelihood that there are different religions in your room. You may opt to go more toward a seasonal theme, like winter.

September
- Schoolhouse
- Summer fun. Display pictures of places students went over the summer.
- Apples ("You're the Apple of my Eye.") Tree with apples. Write each student's name on an apple, take individual pictures the first day of school and place on the apples.
- Two cheerleaders with megaphone sheets. On megaphone have students write information about themselves.

- Tree with multicolored leaves. Put students' names and pictures on leaves. ("Everything Is Falling Into Place.")

October
- Witch, scarecrow, or autumn scene
- Write stories about fall, Halloween, Columbus
- Fire safety
- Have students design paper pumpkins, vote on the best design

November
- Turkey (Turkey tales—have story starters on each feather of a turkey—children pick one and complete the story on a turkey ditto.)
- Draw a hand and have students cut out and write what they are thankful for.
- Indians and Pilgrims
- Family—write something about their families, map out family trees.
- Elections
- Facts on previous presidents

December
- Santa
- Display the front of old Christmas cards and have students select one to describe. (As an independent activity, have students match description to card.)
- Elf workshop—task directions written on elf hats, read numerous stories about Elves, Brownies, Trolls, Fairies, Dwarfs to the class
- Winter Sports

January
- Snowman
- Snowflakes
- Winter fun stories or pictures
- Write New Year Resolutions on bells. (Ringing in the New Year.)

February
- Happy Birthday To . . . (write about a famous person born in February)

- Famous Black Americans – research one Black American and write about that person or the contribution he/she made on a heart ditto.
- Heart month – study the heart and how to keep it healthy.
- Dental

March
- Leprechauns, shamrocks – write limericks, or stories about what the leprechaun found at the end of the rainbow, use shamrocks for spelling tests and put on the bulletin board, help the leprechaun with his math facts.
- Kites
- Poison Prevention/Safety

April
- Rabbits
- Food and Nutrition
- Kangaroo (Spring Has Sprung)

May
- Flowers, plants, living things
- Spring Sports
- Storm Safety

June
- Animals
- June Dreams
- Summer plans
- I display a copy of work the child completed in September beside one completed during the last week in May (How We Changed).
- Write about something special they enjoyed doing sometime during the year (Memories).

Other suggestions
- Current events
- Children's writing
- Poetry
- Student of the week (Have students fill out information about themselves – what they like to do, their favorite subject, how many pets they have, and how many family members.)

- Give each student a paper T-shirt to design, hang them up and each week have students pick their best work paper to display under their T-shirt.
- Birthday train
- Make a chart that has students' names on the side and the number of spelling chapters in spelling at the top. Each week allow students to put sticker on if they pass with an A.
- Label a section—"Helpers"—cut out hand shapes and label with a job description, next to it put the student's name who will be doing that job (change names weekly).

Bulletin boards are only one of many jobs that you have to complete. Let students help you as much as they can. There are many good books on the market to give you ideas. This is an area where you may relax and let students assume responsibility. I can guarantee your job will be made easier, and your students will love seeing their products!

6/ Transition Techniques

TRANSITION from one lesson to another is an area where I still have problems. What do you do with those students who finish work early? How do you move smoothly from one lesson to another? How do you prepare, distribute, and collect materials? What do you do with those extra minutes? This chapter is aimed at answering or at least suggesting solutions to these questions. Effective transitions must be made so that discipline problems do not result.

To help students make the transition from one subject to another, try to have a schedule that is basically the same every day. If they know what to expect, they will move more smoothly into the next activity. Summing up the lesson lets students know you are ready to finish and change ideas. Give them a few minutes to make transitions by clearing their desks and getting out what is needed for the next subject. Other effective transitional tips include the following:

(1) Have organized lessons and materials ready.

(2) Look for students who may be upset and talk to them before beginning the lesson. This gives you the chance to reverse a possible problem later on.

(3) Be consistent in expectations to maintain good behavior at all times.

Now to answer the question, what do you do with those students who complete work quickly? This is an area where I had problems after switching from nursery school to third grade. I found that I could give an assignment and within ten minutes, two to three students would be done. If I tried to give them something to do, they thought it wasn't fair that they had to do "extra things." It took me a while to work out a solution, but below is a list of things students could choose.

- projects – anything the child is interested in and would like to learn more about (great for research)
- silent reading
- creative stories
- finish up other work not completed
- on certain days – games
- drawing
- tutor slower children
- choice of learning centers
- run errands, do room chores
- correct papers
- manipulatives
- puzzles
- arts and crafts
- work on lesson to present to the class
- SRA reading or math kit

I found it much easier toward the end of the year because I had built up a repertoire of things from which students could choose. Instead of giving them something to do, the choice was given back to them. Given the opportunity to choose, students had the incentive to work on extra things.

When it comes to preparing materials, many teachers find it easier to work on them over the summer. Once school starts, you have lessons to teach, papers to correct, and meetings to attend. Do as much as you can before September, and the time you save will please you.

As you get ready to distribute materials, let students help you. My students sit in groups, and I have group leaders who are responsible for getting materials for their group. I do not wait for papers to be distributed, as this creates time for students to misbehave. I begin reviewing what was taught yesterday, and by the time papers are passed out, I'm ready to start the lesson. Another teacher suggested having pamphlets of that day's work and putting them on student's desks before they arrive. Material could be put out before students arrive and they could collect it before going to their desks. Remember, you cannot hand out materials one at a time and expect the whole class to remain quiet.

Once papers have been completed, I have folders with students' names on them where they put their work. I cannot tolerate a messy, cluttered desk and found after the second week of school that I could not have the students put their papers on my desk. They were all over the place. Folders cleared up the problem immediately. I had a small table with the folders in a basket, and a spot for workbooks, plus extra credit work. That way everything was in one area. Another way to collect materials is to have a folder for each subject where students can put finished work. I prefer the first method because I can sort papers into piles and know right away who didn't do an assignment.

I also make sure students know where the paper, tape, extra pencils, stapler, and arts and crafts supplies are kept so they do not have to bother me to get them.

Lining Up and Walking in Halls

In most schools students are expected to be quiet in the halls, so they do not bother other classrooms. When you are ready to line up, do not make the mistake I did and have everyone line up at once. Call students by rows, colors, birthday, or any type of listening activity. When you have a couple lining up at a time, you can control the class and maintain peace and quiet. Students lined up should be quiet or sent back to their seats.

You should let the class know from day one what your expectations for hall behavior are, as well as the consequences when these expectations are not met. For the first couple of weeks, if students are noisy in the hall, have them go back to the classroom and start all over. Noisy halls show disrespect for other classrooms; students must be taught to show respect for others! Make a game out of walking in the hall. Students could pretend to be mice who don't want the cat to hear them, or they could be soldiers. Appoint captains for the week, and have those leaders control the noise in the halls. Don't get in the habit of saying—"Shh!" This is not really a way to establish control. The end of the line is usually noisier than the front, so I walk at the end. Then I can see everything that is going on in front of me. I have students stop at corners, just to make sure they are being quiet and we are keeping together as a group. Responsibility is the key to self-discipline; noisy halls, or rooms, are direct reflections on a teacher's ability to control his or her class.

What to Do When You Finish Early

There will be times when you finish a lesson early or have extra minutes. What do you do? You certainly can't leave it to the class to entertain themselves. Below are some suggestions given to me that are favorites of teachers interviewed:

(1) Flash cards—math skills, spelling, vocabulary words

(2) Simon Says—listening skills

(3) Map skills—Have students come find states, rivers, mountains, on maps either at their desks, or on a room map.

(4) Review spelling words—Pick individual students to spell words, or use slates where everyone can write the words (slates are effective for quick review).

(5) Read to students. (When reading, use different voices for the characters and vary in tone—children love it!)

(6) Pantomime reading vocabulary words.

(7) Create a poem about the day.

(8) Around the world using math facts—Begin by pairing two students against one another. Show a flash card; the first one to answer correctly moves on. (Winner is the student who makes it past all the other students, therefore has gone "Around the World.")

(9) Mum ball—Students sit on top of their desks and pass a nerf ball to one another. (Rules—No talking, the person throwing the ball must throw so that the other person can catch it. No one can move from the desk top; otherwise they are out and must sit in their seat.)

(10) Spell-O—Put all the spelling words on the board; students write down any four. Choose one student to go to the board and slowly begin checking off one word at a time (any order); students at their seats check off any time a word is given on their papers. When all four words are called the student stands up and says "Spell-O." He/she gives the list to the person at the board and must correctly spell each of the four words; if the student does this, then he/she can be the person at the board.

(11) Do stretching exercises or aerobics.

(12) Moral discussions—Make up a story and have students discuss

solutions. (Example: You find a wallet on the playground. Inside is a $10.00 bill, just the amount you need to finally get the bike you have been saving to get for months. No one is around to see you if you take the money. You really want the bike! What do you do?)

(13) Sing action songs—Hokey Pokey, Bingo or even camp songs

(14) Make lists—How many different things are made of circles, squares? Give a word and ask students to come up with as many different words as they can which mean the same or opposite thing.

(15) Seven-up—Seven students stand in the front of the room while the rest of the class is seated with heads down, eyes closed, and one hand fisted with the thumb up on desks. The seven students go among classmates, each one pushing a thumb down. They return to the front of the room, and the teacher says, "heads up." Those students that were touched must stand and try to guess who touched their thumb. If they guess correctly, they replace the person who touched them. The game continues until everyone has had their turn to participate, or until allotted time is over.

(16) Describe things or people in the classroom and have students guess what or who it is.

(17) Start with a sentence (Example: "I went to the store and bought . . ."). Each student must add something and repeat what everyone else has said previously.

(18) Brainstorm various topics such as current events (discuss things students have heard on TV/radio), school problems, suggestions for upcoming projects or units.

(19) This is similar to *Wheel of Fortune*—Box out a number of letters on the board. Ask one student at a time for a letter; the one who gives a letter has a chance to guess the character (usually from a book that is being read at the time). You fill in the letters, and the student who does guess can do another character on the board.

(20) Concentrate game—Students list things by the alphabet. The first student begins with letter "a" (e.g., apple), the next one repeats "apple" and gives a word that begins with "b," and so on. Different categories can be used.

(21) Baseball—can be used with flash cards, spelling words, or other

subjects. Divide the class into two teams. Flash a card to the student, and he/she is given three seconds to answer. If the student answers correctly, he/she goes to "first base" (a designated spot). The next student follows the same procedure and goes to first, while first goes to second, and so on. An incorrect answer is an out, three outs and the other team is "up." Score by getting a player "home."

(22) Basketball—This also can be used with math facts, or spelling words. Divide into two teams. The first player up is flashed a card or given a spelling word to spell and use in a sentence. A correct answer earns one point. If answered correctly, the player gets to throw a nerf ball into a wastepaper basket. If the basket is made, it is worth two points. The teams rotate twice.

(23) Guess my word—Place the beginning letter of the word you want students to guess on the board. Divide into two teams. Give a definition of the word from the dictionary and allow teams to guess what the word is.

(24) What's the missing word?—Put a sentence on the board, but leave out a word. Put only the beginning letter on the board. Divide into two teams and have teams come up with a word that could be used correctly in the sentence.

(25) Computer games

(26) On three-by-three cards, write questions to important concepts covered, pass out and have students answer. If you write answers on the back of the cards, students can use these as individual reinforcement.

(27) Write a number on the bulletin board, have students stare at it for 5–10 seconds, then erase. Have individual students guess the number. (I do 8–10 digits for third graders.)

(28) Begin a story and then go around the room having each student make up the next part when it is their turn.

(29) Make cards to cheer up people at nursing homes or hospitals. If time permits have students write a quick note to go along with it.

(30) Students usually love to draw. Give them a topic and let them go to work. (Example: Draw me a picture of a house you would like to live in. Draw me a picture of a pet you would like to have. Draw something you would like to invent.) You could also have

students add a few sentences telling why or describing their drawing.

This is a starting point from which you can begin selecting ideas. Exchange ideas with other teachers, and allow students to come up with some suggestions. You will find your classroom runs more smoothly if you develop a repertoire of ideas to use during those "extra" minutes.

7/////Record Keeping, Documentation and Pupil Files

THE consensus among teachers who have taught for one year or twenty years is that record keeping and documentation is one of the most demanding aspects of teaching, because of the amount of paperwork involved. Efficiency here increases accountability, energy, and teaching time. This chapter covers plans for recording data and documentation, techniques for producing accurate and informative report cards, plus ideas to use when a child may need to be retained. The latter part discusses information contained within student files, how to use it, and what to include during the year.

Record Keeping

Keeping data properly recorded and organized is difficult until you come up with a system that works well for you. Until you get some experience, you may have a hard time deciphering what is important enough to record. I do a lot of record keeping in pencil, because it is much easier to erase than pen. (And that first year is one where you make lots of mistakes!)

The Attendance Register

Now then, let's begin with the attendance register. It is easier to write students' names in after the first week of classes, to accommodate new students who register that week and those who moved but didn't get their names removed from the class list. This will eliminate scribbling out names and help keep everything in alphabetical order. Check with another teacher to see if there is a specific way in which your school mandates attendance registers to be completed. Some schools use checkmarks; others use symbols. However you fill it in, it is usually your responsibility to keep track of all illegal and legal absences, and illegal and legal tardies. Keep track of what excuses count as legal and illegal, as you will have to record these numbers on report cards and permanent record cards.

It is very important you stay on top of what you are doing, because some schools will not let you collect your last paycheck, until your register balances with that of the office. I devised a method where I keep an index card on each student and use a different colored pen for each marking period. I paperclip excuses, in order, to the back of the index cards and write on the cards, the date and reason (e.g., legal/health, illegal/vacation) why the student was absent or tardy. I still fill out the register, but have found this method an easy way to check should any discrepancies arise.

I find that an easy way to take attendance on a day-to-day basis is to make a chart with all the students' names written on individual envelopes. Students are responsible for marking themselves "here" by placing an index card in their envelope. I have smiles and seasonal stickers placed at the top of the index card, so when placed in the envelope, they show. (See Figure 7.1) This is a quick method for taking attendance, and allows students to assume responsibility.

After the first week of school, I make a master copy (see Figure 7.2) with names in alphabetical order and columns, and run off several copies. I use these in a variety of ways:

(1) I use one for each subject for grade recording, because I have more room at the top to write the type of assignment, and jot down any notes I wish to include.

(2) At the beginning of the year there are many forms to be signed by parents and returned, money to be collected for workbooks, *Weekly Reader*, snack milk, and permission slips. It is much easier to check off the appropriate column as things are returned. This is much easier to quickly see who needs to return what.

(3) If you use SRA reading or math kits, it is easy to check off the color and number as completed.

(4) Be creative—you will figure out many uses for this form!

I make another master copy with five columns for each school day (see Figure 7.3), and again, the names are written in alphabetical order.

ATTENDANCE CHART						
SARA		KATE		JERRY		LORI
	MIKE		BILL		SUE	
CASEY		CARLEY		BETHANY		RON
	JOSH		RANDY		ROBIN	

Figure 7.1 Attendance chart.

Names											
Bell, Sue											
Hall, Mike											
Kope, Lori											
Rogers, Brandon											

Figure 7.2 Name chart.

Names	Mon.	Tues.	Wed.	Thurs.	Fri.
Bell, Sue	S R M L				
Hall, Mike	S M				
Kope, Lori	R M L				
Rogers, Josh	S R M L				

Figure 7.3 Daily record keeping.

I use this one for recording students' work as it is completed correctly. For example, when spelling is completed correctly, I write in "S." I use abbreviations for all subjects taught. At the end of the day I can quickly see which students did not finish assignments, and make sure they take them home to complete. If an assignment is going to take a while to mark, then I pencil in the appropriate abbreviation, and go over it in pen when I have checked it. Students who take assignments home and do not turn them in receive a red circle in that space. This allows me to show parents a weekly chart of incompleted assignments.

Students who have homework receive a pink sheet copy that has each subject written on it, and enough space where I can write the assignment that is due. A copy is shown in Figure 7.4. Students take this pink sheet home, and when all assignments are completed, parents must sign it, and the child brings the sheet and work due back to school. This informs parents of work that is not getting done, and should this child be one who needs to be retained, parents are aware of the situation. This system works best in the lower grades where homework is usually not assigned. The sheet could also be given in the upper grades, however, and as students are given an assignment, they could write it in under the appropriate subject as an organizational method. This, of course, need not be signed by parents, unless you have students who do not turn in assignments on a regular basis.

When recording data, it is important to keep it precise by sticking to the main point; otherwise you will spend too much time writing. Remember, you have more than one or two students; saving time is what you are after.

Report Cards

Marking report cards the first year is difficult, because you want to give accurate grades. The problem is that you have a hard time determining what factors are important enough to grade, and what system will give a good indication of how well the student is doing. Some teachers average class participation, test scores, and special assignments to come up with a final grade. Others mark only on quizzes, tests, and special assignments. It will be up to you to determine what to mark or not mark. For papers you are not grading, you must develop a system to give feedback to students, such as: $+$, ν, $-$, S$+$, S, U,

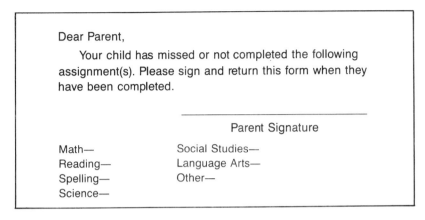

Figure 7.4 Letter to parents.

☺, ☹. Symbols such as these let students know if their papers were above average, average, or below average in quality.

You will have to determine whether you want to grade with letter or number grades. Depending on the level and school system, you may be required to use one or the other. There is an excellent calculator on the market called Grademalic 100 Calculator, put out by Calculated Industries. This averages number and letter grades quickly, converts numeric into letter grades, has a built-in timer, and performs all standard calculator functions. This is a big time-saver, and it is a must for all teachers. One of the third grade teachers at my school showed this calculator at a grade-level meeting, and we all ended up putting this on our requisitions. I have even noticed that one of the book clubs offers this as a selection for redeeming bonus points saved.

When it comes to writing comments on report cards, you should try to include something about academics, work habits, and social skills. This gives parents a brief but informative comment. If you find you have too much to write, then perhaps you need to consider having a conference.

Making Decisions about Retentions

Another hard area for new teachers is how to tell if a child needs to be retained. Retentions occur when a child shows an inability to achieve on the same level as his or her peers. Experienced teachers can tell almost immediately those students who are having problems. Each year over one million students are retained in their current grade. Teachers, principals, and/or parents can make recommendations to retain.

Suggesting to retain a child must be done very carefully, and you must be able to back up your decision with solid, strong reasons why it will be in the child's best interest. To help you in deciding upon your recommendation, I have compiled the following list of factors to take into consideration:

- unacceptable levels of academic achievement (both in the classroom and on standardized test scores)
- the child's chronological or mental age (younger than peers)
- emotional growth levels (the child displays immaturity)
- attendance and general health (high number of days missed or poor health when in school)
- previous school history (child's permanent records show that he/she has struggled in previous grade levels)
- child shows lack of responsibility and poor organizational skills
- child does not participate in group discussions or pay attention during lessons
- poor work habits (desk is not organized; work is not completed on time or lacks information; work is messy; child is off-task most of the time)

If you are the one making the recommendation to retain, make sure you have looked at all the factors involved. It is usually *severe* deficits in one or more of these areas that warrant retention. Each child needs to be considered individually. Do not base your decision on just a couple of factors or incidences that have occurred throughout the year! Check the child's permanent records, discuss the situation with previous teachers and make sure all possible chances of this child succeeding enough to pass have been exhausted.

Realizing this is a tough area for teachers, I have decided it is helpful to discuss two case studies of children who have been retained. Due to the nature of material being discussed and those involved, names and grade levels will remain anonymous.

The first child is a boy who started the school year at a young age due to a birthday in late November. He had a very rough time keeping up with the rest of the class, and cried when material was too hard to do. Realizing right away that there were problems, and that academic material which should have been mastered the year before was not, the first few weeks of review proved to be very stressful for the child. A conference was held during the fifth week of school with the parents to discuss problems. The parents were very understanding, and said that retention had been discussed the year before but had been decided against because report card grades were passing and standardized test scores were borderline. They volunteered to help at home on material and to keep in close touch with the teacher.

As the year progressed, the child showed increasingly immature behavior, and missed a lot of school in the winter due to poor health. Because of this, work became harder and grades fell to failing. It was evident that there was no way this child could be sent to the next grade level, because the problems displayed throughout the year were too severe. The child was retained with the rationale that "a year of growing time" would help with the crying and other displays of immaturity. It would also allow him to catch up on academic material, and hopefully to have a more positive year socially and academically. Today this child is doing extremely well with above-average work, is well-liked by his peers, and shows no negative effects from being retained. By allowing this child another year, he was able to mature and begin to feel good about himself as he met with success in the classroom.

The next child, a girl, had very poor socialization skills, demonstrated a very sneaky manner, and denied when she had done wrong. She had problems working in groups and finishing her work, was very easily distracted, and wanted to share things irrelevant to the topic being discussed. Study habits and skills were very low. She was unorganized, did not listen attentively, and was totally irresponsible. Standardized testing was borderline in most areas, with reading and language falling beneath. A look into the child's permanent folder showed consistently low standardized test scores and report card grades, plus recurring problems in areas described above. It was also learned that due to many ear infections the child had a slight loss of hearing, which came back to normal after tubes were put in. As you can see it, retention was definitely in the best interest of the child.

Usually by midyear conferences you have a good idea of those students who may need to be retained. It is very important to discuss the possibility of retention with parents during this conference. If you know sooner, then by all means inform parents at that time. Communication with parents concerning their child's progress throughout the year is a critical step in making parents aware of the problem and getting them to accept the decision of retention. Parents must be supportive and comfortable, so that they can break the news to their child in such a way that the child's emotional well-being does not become severely damaged. The process must be handled positively, assuring the child that he/she has not failed and his/her best interest has been taken into account. As a teacher you should never mention retention to any student in your classroom. Some well-meaning teachers have told me that when they were starting out, they would tell students if their work or attitude didn't improve, they would be repeating that grade next year. Telling a child this creates pressure and threatens the child's standing and self-esteem within the classroom.

How retentions are handled in the school by teachers and the principal, and at home by the parents, will make all the difference to the child the following year. I wish that schools would form groups so that students being retained could get together and share feelings about repeating. This would improve social skills and increase self-confidence. The key to retaining students is to give them an opportunity to experience new successes and a year in which to mature. The child must be made to feel good about the situation in order for this to happen.

Two important steps to remember include: (1) Become familiar in September with the retention process in your school. Are there certain steps, factors, or guidelines you must follow? (2) Communication with parents is essential! Give parents the opportunity to help their child at home, or hire a tutor for extra reinforcement. They must be supportive and not in contention with you.

Documentation

Documentation is an area that is very important and should be taken seriously by all teachers. Documentation must be made anytime you suspect that parents or outside help may need to be called, or will aid you in gaining a clearer picture of the child. Documentation allows you to back up what you say with actual proof. It also aids you in evaluations, placements, planning, and referrals of students.

Anecdotal Documentation

Documentation is generally of three types: anecdotal, notes and conference reports to parents, and yearly evaluations. I would like to begin with anecdotal documentation, which includes information on a student's interests, abilities, behavior, personality, and so on. Anything that tells you something about a child is considered anecdotal. Anecdotal documentation helps you see the child as a total person or individual. Through it you are looking beyond test score results or daily work.

To aid me in documenting anecdotal records, I buy the large index cards that come in a spiral notebook, and put each student's name on one. During the day, or at the end of the day, I go through each card and document any of the following:

- incidences involving peers or school personnel (verbal or physical in nature)
- work habits (off-task, unable to complete work, work too hard or easy)
- peer relationships
- strengths and weaknesses
- unacceptable behavior

I do not go into a long, detailed report, but briefly jot down what happened, who was involved, and any other things that will help me remember. I do not just write down the negative things, but if someone has had an exceptional day, done something special, or improved, I make note of it. I try to include a quick note on every student's card. This helps me when I am writing report card comments and conference reports. By the middle of the year, I get away from writing on each student's card, and need to use them only for the purpose of referrals (special education or resource help, psychological problems). I always keep scrap paper handy, or small spiral notebooks to jot down incidences and then transfer them to the index cards. Some teachers prefer to document on a weekly basis, but I find too many things happen within a week and I forget the facts.

This takes time, but I know teachers who have lost their jobs, or have not received tenure, because a parent has backed them up against the wall, and with no written data it is the teacher's word against the parent's. Your job is worth protecting even if it takes a little more time to document!

You may as well know going into the first year that you cannot possibly please every parent. From time to time you find parents who may challenge what you say or how you teach. It does hurt when you are doing your very best for a child and parents make accusations against you. I have been in tears more than once after parents have left conferences. As long as you are doing your best, what more can you do? Don't dwell on the negative parent(s), but on the ones who think you are doing a super job. I know this advice is easy to say but hard to follow; however, you cannot let one parent ruin a year for you. This is why documentation is so important—you have written proof confirming what has happened, or took place.

I have been told by administrators that most teachers worry unnecessarily about coming up against problems concerning documentation. The best advice is to trust your professional judgment, and if you think it is best to document, then do so. Write a note concerning the situation to yourself, and if you notice a trend developing (e.g., the same student is hitting others), then write a quick note to the principal to inform him/her, and call the parents. If you involve parents immediately, they are more willing to work with you. If you don't and their child says you did this or that, they usually don't confront you with the problem, but go to the principal or a board member. If you make no one aware of the situation, you are setting yourself up on the defensive. You are going to have to explain things in a situation that may have become hostile. If you involve the principal and parents right away, then you can tell your side of the story in the appropriate manner. You are a professional—trust your own judgment!

Briefly, documentation is important because:

- You are able to detect any patterns that may be occurring again and again or any situations that may be setting those instances off.
- Documenting provides a total picture allowing you to see overall growth.
- It helps you to record situations just as they happened, and not try to recall from memory something that took place a week or month ago.

Documenting Communication with Parents

The second area to document encompasses any notes and conference reports to parents. Anytime you send home any correspondence to parents, make sure you save a copy for yourself. This is very important, especially if a parent claims never to have received a copy. If the note contains important and confidential information, send it by mail. *Do not throw away anything* you send or receive from parents, even after the school year is over. Problems can still arise even after the close of a school year.

Whenever you confer with parents, you should have a written copy of why the conference was necessary, what transpired during it, and any plans for follow-up. Some school districts mandate that both you and the parents sign the report, and that the parents retain a copy. Again, this is very important to do because you are protecting yourself against any potentially unpleasant situations.

Year-End Student Evaluations

Throughout the year you should be documenting things for the year-end evaluation of students, which is the last area of documentation to be discussed. This is done to see if students have mastered and demonstrated academic skills, proper work habits, social skills, and other necessary requirements for their grade level. I use the sheet I spoke about earlier in this chapter to keep track of mastery of academic skills. I break down the major concepts of each subject expected to be mastered in third grade. For example: Cursive writing is taught, so I put a check under the appropriate letter as it is mastered. By documenting this and other subject skills, I am able to see concrete areas of strengths and weaknesses. I save papers that show difficulties for parents. When I meet with parents and write up the profile sheet on each student, no guesswork is involved. I have all the information needed to prepare accurate evaluations.

I know it probably sounds, throughout this section on documentation, as if you need to be very cautious and watch everything you do and say; it's true—you do! You must look out for yourself, because when push comes to shove, no one else will.

Utilizing Student Files

Before school begins you will receive a folder for each student, which contains all their records to date. These files include a lot of information and, due to time constraints you cannot read everything in them. You must decide what is important and warrants your attention.

Within each folder you will generally find copies of report cards, standardized tests, parent conferences, family and medical history, IQ test results, student profile sheets, a reading folder, school history, and, depending upon your school, other information. Look at the results of IQ and standardized tests, but only to give you an indication of the child's ability. You must look at them objectively, not subjectively. Although children may score extremely high on standardized tests, it does not mean they are actually functioning at that level. Standardized tests give you a profile of the child's strengths and weaknesses. Do not think just because a child has a high IQ score, he or she is going to excel in the classroom. All children can excel; some just have to work harder than others. Other things to look for include: special problems (e.g., psychological—emotional, mental, physical—allergies, handicapped conditions), previous reading level completed, and profile sheet. Make sure you find out the home situation—is it a one- or two-parent home? If the child comes from a divorced home, make sure to check for any court order barring one of the parents from picking up the child.

When I interviewed teachers, they expressed mixed feelings on whether teachers should read previous report card grades and comments written by other teachers. I personally do not believe teachers should, because they come away with a preconceived notion of what to expect from that child. If you feel you must look at such records, wait until the first month is behind you. This way you may be pleasantly surprised by some students who are achieving higher than previous records show. If you expect students to do their best, most of them will. They want to please you and will go out of their way to achieve to your standards. Positive encouragement can change a child's life, especially if no one has ever believed in that child before! (I do recommend checking with the school nurse for allergies or medical problems of incoming students.)

Throughout the year you will accumulate things to put in each child's folder. Some teachers prefer to put things in as they get them, while others wait until the end of the year. I find it easier to keep up with the folders on a regular basis. This alleviates the burden of important information becoming lost, and the hassle of just one more thing you need to do that last week of school.

Check with the main office at the beginning of school to see if they have a checklist of items to be included in each folder. In the school system where I work, the following items must be filed for each student:

- report card
- standardized and IQ test results, plus booklet
- student profile sheet
- reading tests
- results of any state-mandated tests
- parent conference write-ups
- documentation of any kind
- notes written to or from parents (especially those who are known to cause problems)
- papers that show problems for any child who is going to be considered for resource or special education
- academic weaknesses that deserve special attention or reteaching the following year

Each school has its own checklist, but the above is a basic idea of various things that are generally included. Whatever you do, *do not* put anything in a child's folder that may be offensive in any way! If you do, you may find yourself in the midst of a lawsuit for slander. With information that you are unsure of, either ask someone for advice or write "see me" in the folder. This way you are protecting yourself and allowing next year's teacher to come see you where you can verbally share the information. Nothing is in writing, and you can breathe easier, without fearing a lawsuit.

This chapter contains a lot of very important information not covered in college classrooms. I have tried to stress the importance of it all, yet tried to keep it simple so it does not overwhelm you. As with all areas of teaching, find a system that works effectively and efficiently for you.

8/////Personnel and Parent Relationships

AN area overlooked in almost every college course is how to work and get along with supervisors, colleagues, secretaries, custodians, and parents. Even though teaching is a profession where you work mainly by yourself, you still have others you interact with on a daily basis. It is important that you treat all of these people equally. If there is anything I cannot stand, it is teachers who place themselves on a pedestal, and look down on others. In order for a school to function and operate smoothly, it takes a network of dedicated individuals working together to create a successful school environment. Everyone is trained specifically for his/her job and must work hard at it. This chapter is dedicated to those individuals, and will provide insight on how to work with them.

Secretaries

Usually the first people you come in contact with are the school secretaries. As far as I am concerned, they have one of the most difficult jobs in the school. Talk about keeping harmony, they do it, and still manage to smile. Their job description includes—typing and running off all forms, ordering and checking in supplies, pupil attendance, entering and deleting students, answering phones, sorting mail, handling passes and lunch loans, updating handbooks, and the list could go on and on. The school secretaries I spoke with said they wish teachers would ask when they don't understand something, instead of attempting to do it on their own. They said many teachers do not follow directions (sounds familiar) and therefore hand in forms done incorrectly. This holds secretaries up and delays deadlines. Don't wait until the last minute to ask for something. Give the office proper time. Teachers need to be organized, to think and plan ahead; this helps take pressure off the help in the office.

The Custodian

Another person you want to acquaint yourself with right away is the head custodian. He/she deserves our utmost respect, for our classrooms would not be nice and clean when we open our door every morning without their dedication. I spoke with several custodians and asked them what bugged them most about working with teachers. Rooms that are messy, poorly organized, and cluttered topped the list of complaints. These rooms are very hard to clean. Teachers who want something done and done immediately are not held in high regard. Finally, custodians are very bothered by those teachers who wait until the last minute and then decide to work in their rooms when the building is getting ready to close. Again, this relates to poorly budgeted time.

Colleagues

From what I have seen myself and heard from other teachers, some of the hardest people to get along with are our colleagues. We are not taught to interact with other teachers, because in our job we are really autonomous. As teachers we are basically self-employed, so when we shut the door to our classrooms, we become the boss. As bosses we do not know how to exist outside of our classrooms. We gossip, criticize, complain, and find fault with those we work with. Teachers need to be stroked—positively. Smile, and let other teachers know when they did a good job with something. Don't compare yourself with other teachers, as this is sure to damage relationships. Be friendly and yourself at all times. Whatever you do, *do not* talk about anyone you work with! The effects of this, if caught, can be long-lasting and even irreversible.

Supervisors

Supervisors (e.g., principals, superintendents) are usually the people we try our best to please—sometimes at the expense of others. Many times we forget that supervisors are people, too. The supervisors I spoke with said one of the hardest areas for teachers is learning how to take constructive criticism. Many take it personally, even though it is directed toward their professional ability. Granted, few people like to hear what they are doing wrong, but how will mistakes be corrected? No one is perfect, and by being able to take criticism, we open the door for growth to take place. The key to working with supervisors is not to put on airs, but to go to them immediately for help when a problem arises. Keep them involved with what is happening in your classroom, and invite them to those "extra" activities. Most supervisors miss the contact with students and love to be included. Supervisors are there to help you. Use them as a resource to help you grow in your teaching abilities.

Parents

The last people I want to discuss are the parents, whose children we see every day. For many teachers, working with parents is the toughest problem. Most new teachers lack the ability and willingness to work with parents, because they are easily intimidated by them. As a teacher, you must remember that probably half of your parents had a less than successful experience in school. This has left them with a negative feeling, which has carried over into how they view their child's school experience. They are sometimes quick to judge and attack; therefore it is up to you to make them feel comfortable, involved, and informed. The rest of this chapter will address this, and will offer tips on how to conduct successful parent conferences.

Having taught seven years in a nursery school, I had contact with parents on a daily basis. Listening to what they had to say about our elementary schools was an education in itself. They felt a total lack of knowledge about what was happening in their child's classroom. When they questioned their children about what went on in school, of course you know the reply—"nothing."

I vowed that if I ever taught in an elementary school, I would make every effort to keep parents informed and involved, just as I had in nursery school! When the chance came I kept my word and, based on responses from parents, did what I said I would. I had numerous phone calls and letters from parents thanking me for making them feel a part of their child's school year. Do not let anyone ever tell you that parents do not want to be involved, they do!

Starting with the first day of school, I send a newsletter home weekly. At the end of the day, during our "family meeting," the class as a group writes a short paragraph for the newsletter on what was learned throughout the day. I try to have individual students on the following day word process the paragraph and save it on a computer disk. This enables them to take a more active role in the production of the newsletter. The newsletter also contains information on special events not only in the classroom, but in the school—birthdays, specials, deadlines for assignments due, and other odds and ends, and allows parents to glance daily to see what is happening. (See a weekly insert of this calendar in Figure 8.1.) Suggestions are given on how to reinforce concepts at home. I do this to make sure parents know what has been covered academically. This way no one can approach me and say, "I

JANUARY	Monday	Tuesday	Wednesday	Thursday	Friday
(Spelling words listed) coat boat Cursive— S, R, K	① Art Music Child of the Week— Janelle	② Gym Movie Happy Birthday Sara!!	③ Art Music	④ Computer Gym	⑤ Art Science Exp.—Amy —Cory —Josh
fan pan . . . Cursive— L, V, W -	⑧ Gym Library Child of the Week— Kate	⑨ Art Music Math Test	⑩ Gym Guest Speaker	⑪ Art Book Report Due	⑫ Gym Science Exp.—Ron —Brie —Jim

Figure 8.1 Monthly calendar.

would have made sure Johnny knew his multiplication facts, but I didn't know he was learning them." I save two copies of each newsletter; one I give to the principal, and the other I file away in a folder. (This is valuable protection, in case some parent accuses you of not doing your job.)

I have students suggest names for the newsletter, and everyone votes on their choice. I also encourage students to read the newsletter to their parents, which promotes not only a sharing time, but improved reading skills. You could opt to have students write a short paragraph at the end of the day, staple them together and take them home on Friday.

Newsletters may seem like just one more thing you have to fit in, but it is worth every effort. Happy parents are less apt to find fault with you, because they appreciate the extra work. They can also help reinforce skills at home because they know what is being taught.

Another way to keep parents informed is by sending home a weekly copy of your tentative lesson plans every Friday for the following week. This allows parents to see what is being covered on a daily basis. It gives students who miss school the opportunity to complete the work, because they know the assignments in advance. Lesson plans are a big help to intermediate students in becoming organized.

I encourage parents to participate in room activities. This lets them see firsthand what is happening. I do not have parents in on a daily basis, because from past experience I know some will end up trying to be "teacher." You generally can tell right away which parents to be careful with. I also plan two programs (usually at Christmas and at the end of the year) in the evening so that all parents and family members can attend. This allows all parents the opportunity to see how their children are doing in a school event and setting.

I use room Moms or Dads and find I now could not be without them. They organize all the special activities and parties for you by finding people to supply things or volunteer their time for that project. You may even find at times they are a terrific source of emotional support.

I send home a questionnaire in September for parents to complete and return. This allows me to see first of all who returns the questionnaire, and also allows me to plan projects I could build around parents' talents. I include the following questions:

(1) Do you wish to volunteer in the classroom? If yes, what days and times are best?

(2) Do you have any special hobbies or talents that you could share with the class? If yes, please list.

(3) Would you like to supply items for classroom projects or parties?

(4) Do you have any ideas that you would like to share on ways I could keep you informed and involved on what is happening within the classroom?

(5) Would you like to be a room mom or dad?

I urge parents to contact me personally via a note, phone call, or meeting if a problem arises. An open line of communication must be established if you are going to work with parents. The first year I gave my home phone number, but I have decided, based on experience, to request that parents contact me at school if possible. This allows me to relax in the evening hours, without added school problems.

Many times students' work does not seem to make it home. I would suggest keeping work until Friday, having students make a cover, stapling the work together, and then send it home. This way it is all in one pile and neater to glance through.

Parent Conferences

At least two times during a school year, offer parents the option of conferring with you. Conducting successful conferences takes experience, patience, and practice. Conferences are very stressful, and they leave you feeling extremely tired. They must be conducted in a professional yet not intimidating way. The following tips were passed on by teachers I interviewed. I hope you find them of some help as you get ready to conduct parent conferences.

(1) Do not compare or mention other students. Parents are there to talk about their child, not other members of the class. Be professional at all times.

(2) Stick to the topic or reason for the conference. By planning an agenda, you will not forget to mention important items. Be prepared!

(3) Most conferences should be no longer than 15–20 minutes, unless there is a serious problem.

(4) Be diplomatic! Wording is very important, because some parents take everything you say personally. Beginning by saying, "I think

you would want to know this . . ." or "I know you may be hurt by this, but . . . ," makes it look as if parents would want to know. This in turn helps them accept it better.

(5) Don't throw so many things at the parents that the most important points become hidden.

(6) Let parents know how much time you have for their conference and what you would like to cover. Gently suggest they may want to wait and hear what you have to say before asking questions.

(7) Don't be all negative; start out with something positive, and leave parents with something positive at the end. A good practice to follow is to give two positives before each negative.

(8) Don't let parents back you up against a wall, therefore causing you to say something you may regret. If you do not know the answer, say so, and tell them you will get back to them later.

(9) Use the phone for conferences to address minor problems.

(10) Try to leave yourself five minutes in between conferences, in case you run over with someone. Be aware that you must run on schedule or you are going to have a line of parents waiting (and believe me this starts out the conference on a sour note).

(11) Do not talk down to parents. You are working with parents to help their child experience success in school. That is your common denominator!

(12) The steps you should follow during the conference include:
- Welcome the parent(s).
- Present purpose of conference and information.
- Allow time for parent(s) to question, share their own information, or make general comments.
- Wrap up.
- End on a positive note.
- After parent(s) leave, quickly jot down any plans for follow up.

(13) Write up all conferences in a report.

All of the individuals discussed in this chapter deserve our support and respect. If you give them this, you should not have as many problems. Be friendly and try to get to know your fellow staff members. Participate in school and social functions. Last and most importantly, remember the golden rule—Treat others as you would want to be treated!

9/////Problems Most Frequently Encountered

MY goal throughout this guide was to offer you suggestions and solutions to real problems you encounter every day, in and out of the classroom. By giving you a reference guide, I hope to save you time trying to find answers to those questions every new teacher has. The time you would normally spend questioning can now be put into increasing your own productivity and effectiveness as a teacher. This chapter addresses some of the problems not discussed in the previous chapters.

Areas of Difficulty

Scheduling

The most overwhelming problem that all teachers have is scheduling. There is not enough uninterrupted time to teach the basics. States are mandating more and more into already crammed curricula, and the people who are suffering are the students. I really have no solution to offer, but I do urge you to take an active role in setting up your own grade-level curriculum. This means meeting with colleagues at your grade level in your district and determining what is required. You may be able to come up with creative ways to integrate various curricula into each other.

Workload

Another problem that many new teachers have is bringing a lot of work home to do. If you are spending numerous hours on schoolwork every night and over weekends, then you are bringing home too much.

If you find you have hours of grading papers and workbooks every night, then you need to let students help with marking. I figure workbooks are exactly that; therefore exchange, or let students who finish early correct them. Use your breaks to grade things. Get to school early and work, because usually you are less refreshed after teaching all day long. Get in the habit of leaving some work at school; take home only what is necessary and important. You must be able to take a break in the evenings, or you are going to find yourself on the way to burnout.

Balancing Advice and Independence

After you have gotten your position, talk to the principal and ask which staff member he or she recommends as someone you can go to with problems and questions. You need to find an experienced teacher you can trust who will properly aid you in the right direction. I have seen some new teachers who ask too many questions, without even attempting to come up with solutions on their own. It is as if they do not trust their own ability to teach. *Do not* do this, because before long you are going to end up like a puppet, doing everything that the person giving the advice does. You are going to make mistakes the first year, but consider them part of the learning process. Sometimes you have to experience failure before you can succeed. Ask for advice *only* if you are really stuck. You must present to others confidence not only in yourself, but in your ability to teach. Remember, you do not have tenure, and do not want to jeopardize it because of insecurities. Every new teacher has questions and problems, but go ahead and experiment, everything will work out in the end.

The Tone of Teaching

Probably one of the toughest problems is setting the tone with students. Every new teacher wants to be liked, and therefore sometimes becomes too "soft." If you are fair, treat students with respect and love, and listen to them, then you are going to have minimal problems. Students will like you. Teach what you feel comfortable with, not what they will like. Students are not going to like everything you must teach, and sometimes they will complain rather loudly about it, but take it with a grain of salt. Did you like learning everything you were ever taught? As long as you are trying to teach things in a professional and interesting manner, smile and tell students you know they may be unhappy, but you have to teach it anyway. (See question number 7 at the end of this chapter.)

Sharing vs. Bragging

Do not go around bragging about what you have taught, or that you have finished the curriculum early. Keep these things to yourself, because many teachers love to gossip, and if these things get back to someone in higher places, you could find yourself in hot water. Once in the beginning of June I said to a colleague that I was in good shape for the end of the year. Somehow it got back to a board member, and the question was brought up at a board meeting as to why some teachers quit teaching in June. I was still teaching, but had all my test scores completed and on records, profile sheets on the students done, along with other odds and ends that must be done by year's end. This is an example of a casual comment getting blown out of proportion. No other teacher needs to know what you are doing in your classroom. You are autonomous; you determine what happens in your classroom. I am not saying you cannot share things, but there is a line between sharing and bragging. Do not cross it.

Working with Slower Students

Also appearing on the list of problems is helping students who are working below grade level. The challenge is not only finding time, but also trying to determine the learning level those students are capable of attaining. Schedules do not allow teachers much opportunity to work with students who are having severe academic difficulties. Using volunteers in the classroom is probably the best solution in working with slower students. Even if you recommend a student for resource or special education testing, it takes months for testing and assessment to occur. Most of the time teachers must teach to the middle group, and unfortunately the slower students are the ones who suffer the consequences.

The Temptation to Go Overboard

Often new teachers seeing and hearing about all the things happening in other classrooms think they must attempt "extra" things, too. They feel they must impress their co-workers. As a new teacher you must remember many of them have been in the field for a long time. They have had the time to develop and add to the basic curriculum. I am in favor of developing extra activities, but do not go overboard. Implement one or two and do a good job. You will not impress anyone or appear competent if you are doing too many extra things. In fact, others will wonder where you find the time to teach academics. In time you will be able to supplement your basic curriculum; just don't do too much too soon! A good rule of thumb is to plan one extra special activity per month.

Student Input

Many times new teachers teach things, but forget they are really teaching *children*. They allow no input, and do not encourage students to become participants. When a question is asked, the first student who raises his/her hand answers it. If answered correctly, the teacher assumes everyone understands and goes on. It is only after giving a test that they realize many students may not have understood. By then it is too late to go back, because you have to keep going forward. A couple of good techniques to use in constantly monitoring all students are:

(1) Have students write the answer to your question on scrap paper or slates, and then hold it up if they got it right. This gives you a quick assessment of the number of students who are understanding and keeping up with your objectives.

(2) Usually the first students to raise their hands are the bright ones. To encourage other students and allow time to think and answer the question, you can say, "Susie's got her hand raised, Johnny does now . . . , ok, now I'm going to pick someone with their hand raised, and Kevin is going to tell us if the answer is right or wrong." Kevin is one of the students with his hand not raised.

This method engages the whole class in the learning process. The students who raise their hands are being reinforced by being noticed, but the students who do not raise their hands, do not know when you will call on them to answer and are therefore being forced to think.

These two methods allow the teacher to monitor learning and then adjust it if needed. The teacher is in control not only of what is being taught but also of what the students are retaining.

The Level of Teaching

Another problem teachers encounter is teaching appropriate material, which means that often teachers teach what students already know. Teachers must find the level where students are currently functioning, and teach from there. Don't assume students know or do not know material. Give a pre-test, or another appropriate method to find out the proper teaching level. Students love to be taught what they already know, because they can turn off and lie back and still get good grades, which results in them learning very little. What good does it do to teach what students already know? On the other hand, you cannot teach above students' heads, or the necessary prerequisites for understanding will not be there.

Knowing the Building

Before school starts, ask someone to give you a tour of the school building. Such things as where the music and art rooms, the gym, auditorium, cafeteria, faculty rooms, and bathrooms are located should be included. Ask what the procedure for fire drills is, and what route you take to exit from your room. Becoming familiar with your surroundings before school starts helps you to better acquaint yourself with the school building.

Further Education

If you are working on a master's degree, check with the business office to see how you get credit for this in your paycheck. Some districts also allow inservice credits to be applied to your paycheck.

Using the Media

When you are doing something special in your classroom, do not forget to use the media as a means of communication. Although this is not a problem, it is an area often overlooked by classroom teachers. Call the newspaper, radio, and television stations. Showing the community what is happening within your classroom is a good means of publicity not only for yourself and your class, but for the school as well. If your school has a community newspaper, regularly write up articles and submit them. Being a teacher means projecting a positive image to the community and allowing others to see the "good" things occurring within our schools.

Some Common Questions

The following questions were ones that new teachers said were important throughout the first year, along with solutions for them.

(1) What do I need to do the first day?

First of all, overplan! Better to have too much than not enough. Secondly, assign desks, cubbies or lockers, classroom helpers, books, and go over rules, procedures, daily and weekly schedules, and fire escape routes.

(2) What type of behaviour should I expect from students during lectures?

Students should be seated at their desks, feet on the floor, attentive, and facing you. There should be no talking and desktops should contain only those items needed for the lesson at hand.

(3) What is the best time for students to sharpen their pencils?

The best time is before you start the first lesson, and right after lunch. Have students sharpen two, in case one breaks. I buy pencils during the back-to-school sales and sell them at cost to students throughout the year. This works well because students always seem to have an extra dime.

(4) What do you do if you need supplies such as, tape, glue, construction paper?

Make a list of everything you must have and turn it in to the office. Some schools have surplus supplies on hand, or will order them for you. Other teachers may let you borrow until you get your own.

(5) The teachers in the teacher's room often talk about other teachers and students. This makes you feel uncomfortable, as they often try to include you in their conversations. How do you handle this?

Teaching can be a lonely occupation for some, so when they go to the faculty room, gossip helps break up the day. If you are very uncomfortable with this situation, you have two choices. One—stay away, or two—just come right out and say you have no opinion on the matter and try to change the subject to safe things (movies, weather, sports). Many times new teachers become discouraged and their spirit becomes dampened by listening to the "politics" discussed in the faculty room. Try to find other new teachers and get to know them—they can be a valuable support group!

(6) How do you deal with a hyperactive child?

Begin by keeping track of when the hyperactivity is being displayed. Does it happen first thing in the morning, getting better as the day goes on? Is it a continuous problem all day? In some cases, cutting out sugar and sweets improves the problem greatly. In other cases it is a physiological problem, and the child may need medicine. Working closely with parents is necessary to get the help the child needs. I had two students in one year who were diagnosed as hyperactive and eventually placed on medicine. The change was substantial, and allowed these children to settle down enough to finish work, pay attention, and pass third grade. It is very frustrating dealing with hyperactive children and sometimes tries your patience to the limit. You must constantly remind yourself that these children cannot help what they are doing.

(7) How do you answer the question, "Why do we have to learn this?"

If you hear this often in your room, you may need to check your objectives. Are you teaching things students already know? Is the lesson boring to the point no one is listening, and could care less? You cannot possibly make every lesson the very best, but you do need to let students know the what and why of the lesson. Letting them know the value and benefits will help them see the relevance of it. I sometimes teach the lesson and then have students figure out why I have taught them that particular skill. If you are unable to figure out why the lesson is being taught, then perhaps it does not need teaching.

(8) How do you handle students who do not complete homework assignments on a regular basis?

The first step is to make the child's parents aware that their child is not completing assignments as required, and ask for their help. A conference with the parents and child may be needed to discuss the problem. Talking with other teachers may help you come up with solutions. Setting up a behavioral modification plan may also work.

(9) How can you be sure that newsletters, notices, and school work get home to parents?

- I send home newsletters and notices from school in a large manila envelope with the parent's name written on the outside. These envelopes are returned the next day by students. This allows me to know that parents are receiving information.
- I pass back all papers to go home on Friday and have the students make a folder to take them home in. If time does not allow this, I staple all papers together.

(10) What is a good system to use for students who never finish their work and must take it home?

In the younger grades it may be difficult for students to remember at the end of the day what they have or haven't finished. I make a chart that can be copied, which has the days of the week on the top of it, and the subjects on the side. Lines divide each of the subjects and days. After I give an assignment I go to each child who has a chart and write in the work assigned. If a child finishes the work before the conclusion of the day, he/she gives it to me and I cross it off. Any work not crossed off must go home as homework, and be crossed off when finished, by a parent.

(11) What is a good method to get the attention of your students? Below I have listed several good techniques to get you started until you have one that works best with your class:

- whisper
- turn the lights off

- start a pattern by clapping
- have everyone that hears you say "Sh"
- use a bell
- raise your hand and have everyone else do the same
- stand in front of the room with your arms crossed and don't say anything
- play a listening game by saying, "If you are listening, touch your nose, touch your stomach, touch your arm," and so on. Last say, "If you are listening, you are sitting up straight, your hands are folded, and your mouth is closed."

(12) Should five week progress or failing reports be sent home each semester?

I strongly believe in five week reports for all grade levels. This is an excellent way to inform parents if their child is failing or borderline in any areas or has raised his/her grades from failing to passing. Parents may opt then for a conference to discuss the situation and help correct the problem at home. This gives them five weeks to do so. (See Appendix G for an example of a five week report I devised for my use.)

(13) How do you keep bright students challenged?

This is an area that greatly concerns me. Many schools have gifted and talented programs but they are not long enough or not usually offered on a daily basis. I try to use advanced spelling words, challenging math problems, or get the student to do a research project on topics they are interested in. The goal is not to let them sit day after day doing things that they already know, but to get them learning and researching on their own.

Throughout your first year of teaching you will encounter many problems and have many questions regarding things you never dreamed would be part of the teaching profession. If you think of these things as part of the learning process, you will grow in many different ways. Do not be afraid of what you come up against; all teachers have been through it and have survived. At the end of my first year I looked back and realized how much I had grown. I was thankful for the ability to tackle each problem head on, and although I didn't handle everything correctly, I definitely learned perseverance! Just remember the first year is always the worst. It does get better.

10 ///// Final Thoughts

I hope that as you have read this guide you have picked up some suggestions and ideas on where to begin once you get the job, and that you now have a better sense of how to make it through the first year. The first year is extremely tiring and very hectic. You spend a lot of time worrying whether you are doing things right, whether you will cover everything by the end of the year, whether students are really learning what they should, plus much more.

One of the advantages of teaching over other professions is that every year it comes to an end. The worry and stress, the students who test you every minute, mistakes you make—all of it ends with the closing of another school year. You get to start with a clean slate, with new ideas and methods each fall. How many professionals do you know who get to start all over every year?

I find teaching the most rewarding, challenging, and stimulating job around. There are so many milestones and daily successes! When a child looks at you eye to eye, throws her arms around your neck, and says she loves you; when a child finally masters something he has been struggling with; when a quiet child begins to open up and blossom; when students say to you, in effect, "You believed in us, you told us you loved us and really meant it every single day"—there is no substituting for these, and the list could go on and on.

Teaching is what you make it. You have the power to make the school year the very best for your students. You can give them memories to last a lifetime, and they in turn can do the same for you. My first year's class collected money, and surprised me with a plaque the last day of school, which proclaimed me, "Teacher of The Year" for being the "Best Third Grade Teacher." Memories such as those last a lifetime, knowing you made a difference in a child's life, and helped them achieve success beyond their wildest dreams. Parents who thank you and let you know you made a difference in their child's life make teaching worth every headache, every effort you put into it.

Teaching is learning—students teaching you and you teaching them. Don't ever stop believing in children, or causing them to believe in themselves. Life is tough on children today; our world is so fast-paced and competitive. We can be their last hope; their once in a lifetime bright and shining star. Give teaching your best shot, and may teaching be to you what it has been to me—an enjoyable occupation that pays me to have fun, and develop lasting lifetime friendships with students.

Good luck as you begin your first year of what I hope is many years of teaching and educating our future. May your light always shine brightly!

In closing, I would like to share the following poem which was given to me by an elementary principal. The message it contains is very clear and self-explanatory.

THE LITTLE BOY
By Helen K. Buckley

Once a little boy went to school.
He was quite a little boy.
And it was quite a big school.
But when the little boy
found that he could go to his room
by walking right in from the door outside,
he was happy.
And the school did not seem
quite so big any more.

One morning,
when the little boy had been in school awhile,
the teacher said:
"Today we are going to make a picture."
"Good!" thought the little boy.
He liked to make pictures.
He could make all kinds:
lions and tigers,

chickens and cows,
trains and boats—
and he took out his box of crayons
and began to draw.

But the teacher said: "Wait!
It is not time to begin!"
And she waited until everyone looked ready.

"Now," said the teacher,
"we are going to make flowers."
"Good!" thought the little boy,
he liked to make flowers,
and he began to make beautiful ones
with his pink and orange and blue crayons.

But the teacher said, "Wait!"
And I will show you how."
And she drew a flower on the blackboard.
It was red, with a green stem.
"There," said the teacher,
"now you may begin."

The little boy looked at the teacher's flower,
then he looked at his own flower,
he liked his flower better than the teacher's.
But he did not say this,
he just turned his paper over
and made a flower like the teacher's.
It was red, with a green stem.

On another day,
when the little boy had opened
the door from the outside all by himself,
the teacher said:
"Today we are going to make something with clay."

"Good!" thought the little boy,
he liked clay.

He could make all kinds of things with clay:
snakes and snowmen,
elephants and mice,
cars and trucks—
and he began to pull and pinch
his ball of clay.

But the teacher said:
"Wait! It is not time to begin!
We are going to make a dish."
"Good!" thought the little boy,
he liked to make dishes,
and he began to make some
that were all shapes and sizes.

But the teacher said, "Wait!
And I will show you how."
And she showed everyone how to make
one deep dish.
"There," said the teacher,
"now you may begin."

The little boy looked at the teacher's dish.
Then he looked at his own.
He liked his dishes better than the teacher's.
But he did not say this.
He just rolled his clay into a big ball again.
And made a dish like the teacher's.
It was a deep dish.

And pretty soon
the little boy learned to wait,
and to watch,
and to make things just like the teacher.
And pretty soon
he didn't make things of his own anymore.

Then it happened
that the little boy and his family

moved to another house,
in another city,
and the little boy
had to go to another school.

This school was even bigger
than the other one,
and there was no door from the outside
into his room.
He had to go up some big steps,
and walk down a long hall
to get to his room.

And the very first day
he was there,
the teacher said:
"Today we are going to make a picture."
"Good!" thought the little boy,

And he waited for the teacher
to tell him what to do.
But the teacher didn't say anything.
She just walked around the room.

When she came to the little boy
she said, "Don't you want to make a picture?"
"Yes," said the little boy,
"what are we going to make?"
"I don't know until you make it," said the teacher.
"How shall I make it?" asked the little boy.
"Why, any way you like," said the teacher.
"And any color?" asked the little boy.
"Any color," said the teacher,
"If everyone made the same picture,
and used the same colors
how would I know who made what,
and which was which?"
"I don't know," said the little boy,
and he began to make pink and orange and blue flowers.

He liked his new school . . .
even if it didn't have a door
right in from the outside!

Which teacher will you be?

APPENDIX A

EXAMPLES OF CLASSROOM SCHEDULES

Kindergarten

8:10 – 8:30	– Morning Meeting
8:30 – 9:00	– Learning Centers
9:00 – 9:15	– Clean-up
9:15 – 9:30	– Sharing Time
9:30 – 10:00	– Reading Readiness Activities
10:00 – 10:15	– Outside or Game Inside
10:15 – 10:30	– Math Readiness Activity
10:30 – 10:45	– Get Ready For Lunch
10:45 – 11:15	– Lunch
11:15 – 11:30	– Read Story
11:30 – 12:00	– Rest Time
12:05 – 12:35	– Specials
12:40 – 1:00	– Recess
1:00 – 1:30	– Enrichment Activities
1:30 – 2:00	– Snack, Independent Reading Time
2:00 – 2:15	– Sum up Day, Read Story
2:15 – 2:30	– Outside
2:30 – 2:40	– Dismissal

First Grade

8:00 – 8:30	– Sharing Time
8:30 – 9:00	– Formal Writing Lesson/Creative Writing
9:00 – 9:30	– Specials
9:30 – 9:45	– Snack
9:45 – 11:40	– Reading Groups
11:40 – 12:00	– Spelling

```
12:00 – 12:30 – Lunch
12:30 – 1:00  – Recess
 1:00 – 1:30  – Math
 1:30 – 1:50  – Gym
 1:50 – 2:30  – Science/Social Studies
 2:30 – 2:40  – Dismissal
```

Second Grade

```
 7:50 – 8:15   – Morning Routine, Announcements, Sharing
 8:15 – 8:35   – Gym
 8:35 – 9:00   – Seatwork
 9:00 – 9:30   – Math
 9:30 – 10:00  – Shared Reading Time
10:00 – 10:15  – Snack
10:20 – 10:40  – Journal Writing
10:40 – 11:45  – Reading Using the Whole Language Approach
11:45 – 12:15  – Lunch
12:15 – 12:35  – Undisturbed Sustained Silent Reading Time
12:35 – 12:50  – Teacher or Student Orally Shares a Book
12:50 – 1:20   – Art
 1:20 – 2:00   – Science/Social Studics/Movies
 2:00 – 2:30   – Playtime
 2:30 – 2:40   – Dismissal
```

Third Grade

```
 8:10 – 8:30   – Spelling
 8:30 – 9:30   – Reading
 9:30 – 9:40   – Snack
 9:40 – 10:25  – Math
10:30 – 11:10  – Gym, Music, or Art
11:20 – 11:50  – Lunch
11:55 – 12:15  – Journal or Silent Reading
12:15 – 1:00   – Language
 1:00 – 1:30   – Social Studies
 1:30 – 2:00   – Science
 2:00 – 2:30   – Recess
 2:30 – 2:40   – Dismissal
```

Fourth Grade

```
 8:10 – 8:40   – Journal – Creative Writing
 8:40 – 9:10   – Spelling Lesson and Assignment
 9:10 – 9:20   – Snack Time
```

9:20 – 10:10 – Math Game (like Multiplication Bingo), Lesson, and Assignment
10:10 – 10:35 – Social Studies Lesson, Activity
10:40 – 11:20 – Special
11:35 – 12:05 – Lunch
12:05 – 12:20 – Sustained Silent Reading
12:20 – 12:50 – Band (for those who are not in band, this is a study hall and playtime)
1:00 – 1:55 – Reading
1:55 – 2:15 – Science Lesson, Activity
2:15 – 2:35 – Language Lesson, Assignment
2:40 – Dismissal

Fifth Grade

8:05 – 8:10 – Attendance, Lunch Count, Flag Salute
8:10 – 8:15 – Announcements
8:15 – 9:05 – Math
9:05 – 10:00 – Specials
10:00 – 11:00 – Reading
11:00 – 11:30 – Science
11:30 – 11:50 – Spelling
11:50 – 12:20 – Lunch
12:20 – 12:40 – Free Time
12:40 – 1:10 – Reading
1:10 – 1:40 – English
1:40 – 2:15 – Social Studies
2:15 – 2:40 – Study Hall – Projects, Homework, Extra Help
2:40 – Dismissal

Sixth Grade

8:05 – 8:10 – Attendance, Lunch Count
8:10 – 8:15 – Announcements
8:15 – 9:15 – Reading
9:18 – 9:58 – Language Arts
10:01 – 10:41 – Math
10:41 – 10:57 – Finish up morning assignments
11:01 – 11:31 – Lunch
11:35 – 12:15 – Science
12:20 – 1:00 – Band and Study Hall or Chorus and Study Hall
1:05 – 1:45 – Social Studies
1:50 – 2:30 – Specials
2:30 – 2:40 – Dismissal

APPENDIX B

120 WAYS TO SAY "VERY GOOD"

1. You're on the right track now!
2. You've got it made.
3. That's right!!!
4. Super!
5. That's good.
6. You're doing a good job!
7. Exactly right!
8. That kind of work makes me very happy.
9. That's really nice.
10. It's a pleasure to teach when you work like that.
11. I'm very proud of you!
12. That's it!
13. You're really improving.
14. Superb!
15. Good remembering!
16. Terrific
17. Outstanding!
18. That's the best ever.
19. That's great
20. You've got that down pat.
21. You remembered!
22. You figured that out fast.
23. I think you've got it now.
24. You're doing beautifully.
25. That's better than ever.
26. You've got your brain in gear today.
27. Tremendous!
28. Fantastic!

29. Keep up the good work.
30. That's the way to do it!
31. That's quite an improvement.
32. You haven't missed a thing.
33. That's the way!
34. That's not half bad!
35. Wow!
36. Right on!
37. Well look at you go!
38. Good for you!
39. Good going!
40. I like that.
41. You outdid yourself today!
42. Marvelous!
43. You did a lot of work today!
44. Keep it up!
45. Good!
46. Now you have the hang of it!
47. Way to go!
48. You're doing fine!
49. I've never seen anyone do it better.
50. You certainly did well today.
51. You are really learning a lot.
52. You did that very well.
53. Now that's what I call a fine job.
54. Nice going.
55. You must have been practicing!
56. That's better!
57. Wonderful!
58. Nothing can stop you now!
59. Now you've figured it out.
60. Now you have it!
61. You are very good at that.
62. Congratulations!
63. You've just about got it.
64. You're really working hard today.
65. I'm proud of the way you worked today.
66. That's coming along nicely.
67. That's very much better!
68. One more time and you'll have it.
69. You really make my job fun.
70. That's the right way to do it.

71. Not bad.
72. Great!
73. Good work!
74. I'm happy to see you working like that.
75. You are doing that much better today.
76. Keep working on it, you're getting better.
77. That's the best you have ever done.
78. A job well done!
79. Good for you!
80. Couldn't have done it better myself.
81. You're getting better every day.
82. I knew you could do it.
83. You did it that time!
84. Sensational!
85. Perfect!
86. Fine!
87. Much better!
88. That was first-class work.
89. Excellent!
90. You're really going to town!
91. You've just about mastered that!
92. Keep on trying!
93. Good thinking!
94. You are learning fast.
95. Now you've figured it out.
96. You make it look easy.
97. Congratulations. You got (   ) right!
98. That's a good (boy/girl).
99. The best.
100. Glowing.
101. Hooray for you!
102. Superior!
103. Spectacular performance!
104. That's impressive.
105. Very creative.
106. Beautiful!
107. You must be proud of yourself.
108. That's a good question.
109. That's a good observation.
110. That's an interesting way of looking at it.
111. Very good. Why don't you show the others?
112. I like how you work with others.

113. Today we made great progress.
114. It's fun to teach when you work so hard.
115. I'm happy to see you work like that.
116. This is a good paper—and it's very neat.
117. A couple more times and you'll have it.
118. The second time will be better.
119. I bet your Mom and Dad will be proud of this.
120. I appreciate your effort.

APPENDIX C/

CHECKLIST

Put this checklist in a place where you will run across it again (and again).

- Do I remember to say (both in action and in words) "I like who you are"?
- When I don't like what you do, do I remember to say "I don't like what you are doing" but clearly have it understood that "I still like you"?
- Am I doing things for the children that they can do for themselves?
- Do I give the children choices (the ones I am willing to live with)?
- Am I able to say "I've changed my mind" or "I was wrong"?
- Am I observing what the children like to do and are interested in and follow their lead occasionally?
- Do I make an effort to get inside their minds/shoes for a while, to see things from their point of view?
- Do I make an effort to learn more about the stages of development the children are in?
- Do the students and I brainstorm options, evaluate and make choices together?
- Am I willing to go with group choices when applicable?
- Do I say "I like you"; "I feel happy to share this with you"; "How special our time together is"; "I learn from you"?
- Do I build on strengths?
- Do we play together?
- When was the last time we really laughed together?
- Do I say, "I appreciate . . ."?
- How many times did we touch today? Keep track one day—especially for older children.
- When are the times we sit or talk one on one, eye to eye, heart to heart?

APPENDIX D

LEARNING STYLES

From various educational courses, you have learned that people have many different learning styles. Below are some characteristics of nine common learning styles.

(1) Visual Language—This is the pupil who learns well from seeing words in books, on the blackboard, charts or workbooks. He or she may even write down words that are given orally, in order to learn by seeing them on paper. This student remembers and uses information better if he or she has read it.

(2) Visual Numerical—This pupil must see numbers on the board, in a book, or on a paper, in order to work with them. He/she is more likely to remember and understand math facts when they are presented visually but doesn't seem to need as much oral explanation.

(3) Auditory Language—This is the pupil who learns from hearing words spoken. He/she may vocalize or move his or her lips or throat while reading, particularly when striving to understand new material. He/she will be more capable of understanding and remembering words or facts that could only have been learned by hearing.

(4) Auditory Numerical—This student learns from hearing numbers and oral explanations. Remembering telephone and locker numbers is easy, and he/she may be successful with oral number games and puzzles. This learner may do just as well without his or her math book, for written materials are not important. He/she can probably work problems mentally, and may say numbers out loud when reading.

(5) Auditory-Visual-Kinesthetic Combination—The A-V-K student learns best by experience; doing self-improvement. He/she profits from a combination of stimuli. The manipulation of material along with accompanying sight and sounds (words and numbers seen and heard) will aid

his/her learning. This student may not seem to understand or be able to concentrate or work unless totally involved. He or she seeks to handle, touch and work with what he/she is learning.

(6) Social-Individual—This student gets more work done alone. He/she thinks best and remembers more when the learning has been done alone. This student cares more for his/her own opinions than for the ideas of others. Teachers do not have much difficulty keeping this student from over-socializing during class.

(7) Social-Group—This pupil prefers to study with at least one other pupil, and will not get as much done alone. He/she values others' opinions and preferences. Group interaction increases his/her learning and later recognition of facts. Class observation will quickly reveal how important socializing is to this pupil.

(8) Expressiveness-Oral—This pupil prefers to tell what he/she knows. He/she talks fluently, comfortably and clearly. Teachers may find that this learner knows more than written tests show. He/she is probably less shy than others about giving reports or talking to the teacher or classmates. The muscular coordination involved in writing may be difficult for this learner. Organizing and putting thoughts on paper may be too slow and tedious a task for this student.

(9) Expressiveness-Written—This pupil can write fluent essays and good answers on tests to show what he or she knows. He/she feels less comfortable, perhaps even stupid, when oral answers or reports are required. His/her thoughts are better organized on paper than when they are given orally.

APPENDIX E

DEALING WITH DIFFERENT PERSONALITY TYPES

The following are some typical classroom profiles with some "try this" suggestions.

Aggressive Child

Symptoms

- looks for trouble
- is on the defensive
- blames others
- fights, kicks, hits and picks on others
- bullies
- is quarrelsome
- disrupts class
- destroys property
- "sasses" adults
- is resentful, defiant, rude, sullen

Try This

- Keep the child busy.
- Give big muscle activities.
- Give simple but definite standards of conduct.
- Give child responsibilities.
- Talk with the child quietly.
- Attempt to make friends with the child.
- Help the child to understand and learn to control himself/herself.
- Seek help through professional staff.

"Remember"

- Be calm and patient—improvement will be slow.
- There will be setbacks.
- Overlook more than you see.
- Fighting may give a child immediate relief for pent-up anger or emotions.
- Think over your own feelings and actions toward the aggressor.

Careless Child

Symptoms

- makes many mistakes in school work
- loses or breaks things
- does "messy" school work
- is happy-go-lucky
- has a "don't care" attitude
- misplaces materials

Try This

- Relieve pressures if child is tense.
- Teach the child to better organize time and work.
- Check your classroom standards.
- Talk to parents; learn their attitudes.
- Refuse to accept a paper that is messy, if the child can do better.

"Remember"

- It is easy to be careless.
- A child is a product of his/her environment.
- Careful attitudes come slowly.
- Praise will help.
- A change in standards involves the whole family.

Dirty Child

Symptoms

- has stringy, dirty, uncombed hair
- wears dirty or torn clothes
- needs a bath
- "smells" bad
- uses sloppy eating habits
- smudges papers
- has dirty hands

Try This

- Discuss standards of cleanliness with the class.
- Send the child to wash – quietly.
- Praise the child privately when he/she is neat and clean or if the child makes an effort.
- Seek help for family – contact through professional staff.

"Remember"

- Dirty children can be clean inside.
- It probably isn't his/her fault.
- He/she needs help – not scorn.
- Criticizing the home doesn't solve the problem.

Dishonest Child

Symptoms

- takes things
- steals even though he/she doesn't need the article
- lies when caught
- cheats
- lacks respect for property
- hides things in desk
- puts his/her name on papers others have finished

Try This

- Remove temptations.
- Show the child that you trust him/her, but do not condone dishonesty.
- Discuss the child's problem with him/her.
- Set standards of honesty and truthfulness for the class.
- Arrange classroom setting for closer observation.

"Remember"

- The words "steal" or "lie" should be avoided when discussing the child's behavior.
- It is not good to publicize the child's problem.
- Try to understand the child's motives.
- Dishonesty may be a sign of something more deeply emotional.

Disobedient Child

Symptoms

- is impolite/insolent

- talks back
- pays no attention
- is an "I dare you" type
- wants own way
- rebels against conformity

Try This

- Let the child help build group standards of behavior.
- Give the child special jobs and responsibilities.
- Help the child make his/her own decisions.
- Avoid ultimatums.

"Remember"

- Punishment is not necessarily the answer.
- This kind of child is often a "leader."
- Avoid threats, you may have to deliver.
- Condemn the disobedience, not the child.

Extreme Extrovert

Symptoms

- is non-conformist
- rebels when suppressed
- talks out – impatient
- is positive in statements
- demands center of the stage
- overpowers others verbally and physically
- waves hands to recite

Try This

- Help the child develop socially acceptable skills.
- Praise the child's good points.
- Assign quiet work at his/her desk.
- Assign the child to group activity under another leader.

"Remember"

- He/she needs quiet, calm, understanding help.
- Class pressure may strengthen extrovert tendencies.
- Public admonition gives the child more attention.

Fearful Child

Symptoms

- panics easily – gets frustated
- withdraws
- shows anxiety
- is afraid of being hurt
- fears criticism
- desires constant reassurance
- trembles quickly
- is moody

Try This

- Give sincere love and affection.
- Create activities to release fears.
- Build up the child's confidence.
- Praise the child for accomplishments.
- Help the child to adjust to his/her fears.

"Remember"

- Fears may be imaginary.
- Fears diminish with maturity.
- A child, happy and successful in class, loses his fears.

Lazy Child

Symptoms

- avoids effort – doodler
- is listless, careless
- seldom volunteers
- is sluggish
- daydreams
- does not complete work assignments
- lounges in seat

Try This

- Overlook minor failings.
- Challenge the child.
- Find out if there are health or physical problems.

"Remember"

- Laziness may be a physical deficiency.
- Laziness is an attention-getter.
- Laziness may be an acquired habit.

APPENDIX F

BUILDING STUDENTS' SELF-ESTEEM

I would like to share an idea I developed after finding that students enjoy eating in the room. Each week one student is chosen as "Student of the Week." That student is given a space on the bulletin board to display pictures of family members and him/herself. An autobiography completed during the first week of school is also displayed. Students are encouraged to share or demonstrate any special talents or hobbies they have. One day during the week the student may invite five friends to a "dinner party" at lunchtime. I cover a table with a tablecloth, add a centerpiece and candles (electric if you cannot have an open flame), placemats, turn the lights off, and add any other touches to create the atmosphere of a dinner party. Everyone who attends usually dresses up for the event. I look forward to the dinner parties, because I get the opportunity to share with students on a more personal level. They, in turn, get to see me not just as a teacher, but as a real person with other interests outside of school.

On the day that the "Student of the Week" eats in the room, I have each member of the class complete the following sentence, "_____ is special because _____," and draw a picture. This is something that first needs to be discussed as a large group. What does the word special mean and how are people different and yet unique in their own way? Children are not used to finding these qualities about each other. I am always amazed by the end of the year with what they write about. I collect the completed sheets and staple them in a booklet and entitle it, "_____ is special!!!" The students love both of these activities and really do feel special and loved throughout the week. It is their week to "shine," and for some this may be a rare opportunity.

I also have students make a booklet entitled "All About Me" the first week of school. This is a great way for students to read about their classmates, and for me to gain more of an insight about each individual child. I use the following questions in the booklets but you may come up with some more appropriate for your grade level:

My full name is _____.

I am _____ years old.

I was born on _____.

My address is _____.

My phone number is _____.

I have _____ people in my family.

My favorite place is _____ because _____.

When I grow up I want to be a _____.

I would like to be better at _____.

My favorite game or toy is _____.

I like to spend money on _____.

I am unhappy when _____.

The best thing that could happen to me is _____.

At school I am _____.

I think school is _____.

My favorite color is _____.

I am proud of _____.

On weekends I spend my time _____.

My favorite TV show is _____.

I do not like to _____.

My favorite special is _____.

My favorite subject is _____.

I wish grown ups would or wouldn't _____.

My favorite cookie is _____.

My favorite food is _____.

I think I am really good at _____.

The perfect age is _____ because _____.

I would like to learn _____.

I like to _____.

In _____ grade I wish _____.

THIS IS A PICTURE OF ME.

APPENDIX G

EXAMPLE OF FIVE WEEK REPORT FOR PARENTS

Tully Elementary School Fifth Week Notice

Student _____

Teacher _____ Grade _____

Your child is failing or borderline in the subjects checked below:

_____ Reading   _____ Math

_____ English   _____ Spelling

_____ Handwriting   _____ Science

_____ Social Studies

Areas contributing to problem:

_____ Poor test scores

_____ Working below grade level; lacking appropriate skills

_____ Work is not being re-checked and/or sloppy

_____ Poor attitude toward school and work

_____ Assignments are not being handed in

_____ Other:

   _____

   _____

   _____

   _____

If you wish to discuss this further, please contact me.

APPENDIX H

JOURNAL IDEAS

At a time when our nation is talking about the writing skills of our young, many more teachers are incorporating journal writing into their daily schedules. I have students buy a spiral notebook to write in and collect five per day to read, so by Friday I have read each one. Monday through Thursday I write a topic on the board for students to write about (if they can think of a topic on their own I let them do so). Fridays are free days, which means you can write about anything you would like. I normally give students ten to fifteen minutes to write. Due to the fact that I want students to see the importance of journal writing I also keep a journal. I tell my students not to worry about spelling as I am more concerned with their writing and how well they express themselves.

To help you get started I have listed some topics below. I am sure that once you get started you will find many ideas to write about. Be sure to ask the class for suggestions—they are a terrific resource!

Growing Up
My Parents' Dumbest Rule(s)
The Perfect Day
My Best Vacation
My House
Music
What I Received for Christmas
My Family
My Favorite Pet
Allowance
I would like to visit . . .
Friends
My Favorite Cartoon

My Weekend
My Favorite Things
My Favorite Holiday
My Secret Hiding Place
My Bedroom
A Dream I Remember
The worst food is . . .
School
Swimming
I am proud of . . .
Scary Noises
I wish my teacher would . . .

RECOMMENDED READING

Bulletin Boards

Butterfield, S. 1981. *Bulletin Boards.* NY: MacMillan Publishing Company, Inc.
    This book covers borders, calendar ideas, seasons, plus holidays, and skill
    borders for the bulletin board.
Grewe, G. and S. Glover. 1982. *Bulletin Board Smorgasboard.* Santa Barbara, CA:
    The Learning Works Inc.
    Contains ideas and suggested layout of bulletin boards for all subjects.
Quackenbush, L. and W. D. Rasmussen. 1982. *Border Book . . . Creative Writing.*
    St. Louis, MO: Milliken Publishing Company.
    Twenty duplicating masters of border pictures for students to color and stimulate
    creative writing. Contains suggestions for teachers on creative writing ideas and
    story starters.

Classroom Discipline and Management

Dittburner, D. A. and R. L. Garvais. 1985. *What do you do when—?: A Handbook for
    Classroom Discipline Problems with Practical and Positive Solutions.* Lanham,
    MD: University Press Of America.
    Deals with classroom management problems and solutions. An invaluable re-
    source!
Kreidler, W. J. 1984. *Creative Conflict Resolution—More than 200 Activities for Keep-
    ing Peace in the Classroom K–6.* Glenview, IL: Scott, Foresman & Company.
    Contains over 20 conflict resolution techniques with examples, 14 reproducible
    worksheets, and over 200 class-tested activities and cooperative games.
Lickona, T. 1983. *Raising Good Children.* New York, NY: Bantam Books.
    Even though this book is written for parents, it is an outstanding resource on
    moral development from birth to adulthood. A must for teachers!
Lickona, T. 1991. *Educating for Character.* New York, NY: Bantam Books.
    How to teach general positive values in the school classroom.

Learning Centers

Forte, I. and J. Mackenzie. 1972. *Nooks, Crannies and Corners, Learning Centers for Creative Classrooms*. Nashville, TN: Incentive Publications, Inc.
Uses question-answer format in relating to individualized teaching and the learning center approach. Highlights classroom management, student assessment, record keeping, and use of teacher-made and commercial materials.

Forte, I., M. A. Pangle and R. Tupa. 1973. *Center Stuff for Nooks, Crannies and Corners*. Nashville, TN: Incentive Publications, Inc.
Contains more than 50 ideas for learning centers in language arts, science, social studies, and math.

Lloyd, D. 1974. *70 Activities for Classroom Learning Centers*. Danville, NY: Instructor Publications, Inc.
Describes what learning centers are, how they are used, plus criteria, organization, and management of them. Lists activities for each subject.

Miscellaneous

Alexander, R. 1986. *Instructor's Big Book of Absolutely Everything: 1001 Great Ideas to Take You through All Year*. Nashville, TN: Incentives Publications, Inc.
A spiral book that gives ideas for year-round planning in areas such as: basics, computers, bulletin boards, relationships, seasons, and crafts.

Colvin, M. P. 1978. *Instructor's Big Basics Book*. New York, NY: Instructor's Publications, Inc.
This contains Instructor's magazine 55 best master plans for teaching the basics. Over 100 reproducible ready-to-use classroom activity sheets are provided.

Darrow, H. F. 1986. *Independent Activities for Creative Learning*. New York, NY: Teachers College Press.
A handbook designed to develop critical thinking skills through individualized and small group instruction. 110 independent activities are included.

Forte, I. 1989. *Teacher-Tested Timesavers*. Nashville, TN: Incentive Publications, Inc.
A must for teachers! Contains hundreds of ready-to-reproduce materials such as: awards and certificates, monthly calendars, charts, forms, records, and much more.

Fredericks, A. and E. LeBlanc. 1986. *Letters to Parents*. Glenview, IL: Scott Foresman & Company.
A valuable aid for enriching children's reading experiences. Contains over 200 ideas for building reading skills and provides forty ready-to-duplicate letters with reading activities for parents to do at home.

Liu, S. and M. L. Vittitow. 1985. *Learning Games Without Losers*. Nashville, TN: Incentive Publications, Inc.
A unique book that offers over forty non-competitive learning games to students with varying degrees of abilities.

McDonald, M. 1971. *Teacher's Messages for Report Cards: Suggestions & Examples.* Belmont, CA: David S. Lake Publishing.

Helps teachers write more effective comments for common school problems. Problems are broken down and categorized; for example—behavior problems, weak, slow and immature work, year-end messages, and many more.

Michener, D. and B. Muschlitz. 1983. *Filling The Gaps.* Nashville, TN: Incentive Publications, Inc.

Contains eighty activities for those extra moments you have to fill and have nothing planned.

Nelson, P. 1986. *Teacher's Bag of Tricks.* Nashville, TN: Inventive Publications, Inc.

Provides 101 instant activities in language arts, math, science, plus brain teasers, monthly art, and class room enrichment projects.

Petreshene, S. S. 1985. *Mind Joggers! 5- to 15-Minute Activities That Make Kids Think.* West Nyack, NY: Center for Applied Research in Education, Inc.

Designed to fill time gaps with quick activities in thinking and reasoning, math, language and writing, and listening and remembering. Contains over 150 total group, partner, and individual activities.

Reading and Writing

Boote, R. and R. Reason. 1986. *Learning Difficulties in Reading and Writing: A Teacher's Manual.* Windsor, Berkshire: The NFER-NELSON Publishing Company, Ltd.

Includes specific assessment procedures, record keeping and instructional sequences, plus real case studies.

Frank, M. 1979. *If You're Trying to Teach Kids How to Write, You've Gotta Have This Book!* Nashville, TN: Incentive Publications, Inc.

Provides teachers with ideas and sources for motivation of writing.

Science

Levenson, E. 1985. *Teaching Children about Science: Ideas & Activities Every Teacher and Parent Can Use.* Englewood Cliffs, NJ: Prentice-Hall, Inc.

Science concepts are divided into 10 topic chapters, which are broken down into sequential activities and ideas. Activities come complete with materials needed, procedure, suggested questions to ask and vocabulary to develop, plus why the activity was done and the expected outcome.

Peeples, S. L. and D. L. Seabury. 1987. *Ready-To-Use Science Activities for the Elementary Classroom.* West Nyack, NY: The Center for Applied Research in Education, Inc.

This resource, developed for grades 3–8, contains interdisciplinary activities, teacher-directed activities and aids, and over 130 reproducible student activities for science curricula.

Whole Language

Whole language is an approach that is gaining in popularity. Research has been going on for more than twenty years, and whole language teaching has been found to be very successful in many countries around the world. The philosophy behind whole language is that, by using an integrated approach, children learn to read by reading, while being exposed to writing, speaking, listening, doing, and thinking. Subjects are not isolated, but intertwined so they are interdependent. Language is best learned when used in authentic situations that have meaning to the learner. Whole language teachers, besides believing that children learn to read by reading, view reading as a developmental process.

Reading must be made meaningful to children to be successful. Have you tried to read and retain material that was not meaningful to you? Reading is more successful when it is tied into the other languages (writing, listening, speaking, illustrating), and when all modes of learning are used (auditory, visual, and kinesthetic).

Teachers who use this approach are not tied into reading groups, basals, workbooks, or dittos. Students end up developing a love for literature. The following list of reference books was given to me by a first grade teacher who believes whole language is the only way. I have not yet used this approach, but after talking with teachers who do use it, and seeing their enthusiasm, I plan to do so immediately!

Atwell, N. 1987. *In The Middle*. Portsmouth, NH: Heinemann Educational Books.

Butler, A. and J. Turbill. 1984. *Towards a Reading/Writing Clasroom*. Portsmouth, NH: Heinemann Educational Books.

Calkins, L. 1983. *Lessons from a Child*. Portsmouth, NH: Heinemann Educational Books.

Calkins, L. 1986. *The Art of Teaching Writing*. Portsmouth, NH: Heinemann Educational Books.

Clay, M. 1975. *What Did I Write?* Portsmouth, NH: Heinemann Educational Books.

Goodman, K. 1986. *What's Whole in Whole Language?* Portsmouth, NH: Heinemann Educational Books.

Goodman, K., Y. Goodman and W. Hood, eds. 1989. *The Whole Language Evaluation Book*. Portsmouth, NH: Heinemann Educational Books.

Graves, D. 1983. *Writing: Teachers and Children at Work*. Portsmouth, NH: Heinemann Educational Books.

Graves, D. and V. Stuart. 1985. *Write from the Start*. New York, NY: E.P. Dutton.

Hansen, J. 1987. *When Writers Read.* Portsmouth, NH: Heinemann Educational Books.

Harste, J., K. Short and C. Burke. 1988. *Creating Classrooms for Authors.* Portsmouth, NH: Heinemann Educational Books.

Hornsby, D., D. Sukarna and J. Parry. 1986. *Read On: A Conference Approach to Reading.* Portsmouth, NH: Heinemann Educational Books.

McCracken, R. and M. McCracken. 1972. *Reading is Only the Tiger's Tail.* San Rafael, CA: Leswing Press.

McVitty, W., ed. 1986. *Getting it Together: The Reading-Writing Classroom.* Rosebery, NSW, Australia: Printery Pty. Ltd.

Newman, J. 1984. *The Craft of Children's Writing.* Portsmouth, NH: Heinemann Educational Books.

Newman, J., ed. 1985. *Whole Language, Theory in Use.* Portsmouth, NH: Heinemann Educational Books.

Parry, J. and D. Hornssby. 1985. *Write On: A Conference Approach to Writing.* Portsmouth, NH: Heinemann Educational Books.

Rhodes, L. and C. Dudley-Marling. 1988. *Readers and Writers with a Difference.* Portsmouth, NH: Heinemann Educational Books.

Routman, R. 1988. *Transitions: From Literature to Literacy.* Portsmouth, NH: Heinemann Educational Books.

Turbill, J., ed. 1983. *No Better Way to Teach Writing.* Rosebery, NSW, Australia: Bridge Printery Pty. Ltd.

Trelease, J. 1985. *The Read-Aloud Handbook.* New York, NY: Viking Penguin Inc.

BIBLIOGRAPHY

Barufaldi, James P., et al. 1985. *Heath Science—Level 3*. Lexington, MA: D.C. Heath and Company.

Canter, Lee and Marlene Canter. 1976. *Assertive Discipline*. Santa Monica, CA: Canter & Assoc., Inc.

Carter, Ronald D. 1972. *Help! These Kids Are Driving Me Crazy*. Champaign, IL: Research Press.

Davis, Jean E. 1974. *Coping with Disruptive Behavior*. Washington, DC: National Education Assoc.

Evertson, Carolyn M., et al. 1984. *Classroom Management for Elementary Teachers*. Englewood Cliffs, NJ: Prentice-Hall, Inc.

Glickman, Carl D. and Charles H. Wolfgang. 1986. *Solving Discipline Problems*. Boston, MA: Allyn & Bacon, Inc.

Hollingsworth, Paul and Kenneth H. Hoover. 1982. *A Handbook for Elementary School Teachers*. Boston, MA: Allyn & Bacon, Inc.

Mager, Robert F. 1975. *Preparing Instructional Objectives*. Belmont, CA: Fearon Pub., Inc.

Rogers, Dorothy M. 1987. *Classroom Discipline: An Idea Handbook for Elementary School Teachers*. West Nyack, NY: Center for Applied Research in Educ., Inc.

INDEX /////

ABOUT THE AUTHOR/////

CINDY Christopher graduated in 1980 with a B.S. in Elementary Education. Upon graduating she opened a nursery school for two- to five-year-olds, which she taught and directed for seven years. She is currently teaching third grade and directing a drama program for fourth through sixth grade students in Tully, New York. Cindy is single and enjoys sports—especially basketball and biking, camping, reading, and the theatre. She is also a lay speaker for the Methodist Church, and a member of Homer Baptist Potter's Clay—a drama ministry group. This is her first book.